PRAISE FOR
IT'S NOT MAGIC

"John Amaechi reflects on his extensive experience and knowledge, and with warmth, kindness, humour and encouragement, translates them into practical strategies and learnable leadership skills. Packed with insightful ideas, reflections and exercises, this book is an invaluable and highly accessible resource, not just for those in leadership, but for anyone who would like to communicate more effectively with the people in their lives."

—**Dr Peter Olusoga,** Chartered Psychologist and host of
The Eighty Percent Mental Podcast

"John Amaechi distils deep personal insight into a practical, accessible guide to leadership. *It's Not Magic* is rich with timeless, actionable advice – especially on communication – that is critical to leadership in any form of organisation. This book will be invaluable for both instinctive leaders and for those for whom leadership feels less natural.

John Amaechi is a powerful voice of challenge when navigating the complexities of modern workplaces. He has a compelling ability to surface the right questions, enabling leadership teams to drive meaningful and lasting change."

—**Sir Robin Budenberg CBE,** Chair of Lloyds Banking Group

"Riveting and important. By expertly and often beautifully demystifying self-awareness and self-improvement, Amaechi makes them superpowers within all our reach."

—**James O'Brien,** broadcaster and writer

"This book dovetails with the state-of-the-art thinking in the academic study of leadership yet makes it approachable for leaders at every stage of development. It really brings the fundamentals of authentic, responsible leadership to life and shows the importance of remembering leadership isn't just about you, it is co-created with the people you lead. This is the magical bit about this book. I am recommending it to everyone I work with."

—**Professor Alexandra Gerbasi,**
PhD, FRSA, Pro-Vice Chancellor and Executive Dean
Faculty of Environment, Science and Economy, University of Exeter

IT'S NOT MAGIC

JOHN AMAECHI

IT'S NOT MAGIC

The **ORDINARY** Skills
of **EXCEPTIONAL** Leaders

WILEY

This edition first published 2026

© 2026 by John Amaechi. All rights reserved.

No part of this publication may be reproduced, stored in a retrieval system, or transmitted, in any form or by any means, electronic, mechanical, photocopying, recording or otherwise, except as permitted by law. Advice on how to obtain permission to reuse material from this title is available at http://www.wiley.com/go/permissions.

The right of John Amaechi to be identified as the author of this work has been asserted in accordance with law.

Registered Offices
John Wiley & Sons, Inc., 111 River Street, Hoboken, NJ 07030, USA
John Wiley & Sons Ltd, New Era House, 8 Oldlands Way, Bognor Regis, West Sussex, PO22 9NQ, UK

For details of our global editorial offices, customer services, and more information about Wiley products visit us at www.wiley.com.

The manufacturer's authorized representative according to the EU General Product Safety Regulation is Wiley-VCH GmbH, Boschstr. 12, 69469 Weinheim, Germany, e-mail: Product_Safety@wiley.com.

Wiley also publishes its books in a variety of electronic formats and by print-on-demand. Some content that appears in standard print versions of this book may not be available in other formats.

Trademarks: Wiley and the Wiley logo are trademarks or registered trademarks of John Wiley & Sons, Inc. and/or its affiliates in the United States and other countries and may not be used without written permission. All other trademarks are the property of their respective owners. John Wiley & Sons, Inc. is not associated with any product or vendor mentioned in this book.

Limit of Liability/Disclaimer of Warranty
While the publisher and the authors have used their best efforts in preparing this work, including a review of the content of the work, neither the publisher nor the authors make any representations or warranties with respect to the accuracy or completeness of the contents of this work and specifically disclaim all warranties, including without limitation any implied warranties of merchantability or fitness for a particular purpose. Certain AI systems have been used in the creation of this work. No warranty may be created or extended by sales representatives, written sales materials or promotional statements for this work. The fact that an organization, website, or product is referred to in this work as a citation and/or potential source of further information does not mean that the publisher and authors endorse the information or services the organization, website, or product may provide or recommendations it may make. This work is sold with the understanding that the publisher is not engaged in rendering professional services. The advice and strategies contained herein may not be suitable for your situation. You should consult with a specialist where appropriate. Further, readers should be aware that websites listed in this work may have changed or disappeared between when this work was written and when it is read. Neither the publisher nor authors shall be liable for any loss of profit or any other commercial damages, including but not limited to special, incidental, consequential, or other damages.

Library of Congress Cataloging-in-Publication Data is Available:

ISBN 9781394338276 (Cloth)

ISBN 9781394338191 (ePDF)

ISBN 9781394338177 (ePub)

Cover Design: Jon Boylan
Cover Image: © Popskraft/stock.adobe.com
Author photo: Courtesy of John Amaechi
Printed and bound by CPI Group (UK) Ltd, Croydon, CR0 4YY

C9781394338276_0210252

To Mum.

CONTENTS

CONTENTS

FOREWORD

When people are really great at what they do, it can seem like magic. We know we've witnessed something remarkable and rare, but we're not always sure how it happened, what was done, or why it made us feel the way it did. If you've ever met or listened to John – and if you haven't, I hope you're able to one day – you will most likely have come away feeling something like that (I suspect that's why you've been drawn to this book). You can sense it, see it, be changed by it — and yet, when you return to the everyday, it can feel like a superb magic trick: powerful, impossible to unpack, and unattainable to the ordinary person.

And yet, we know that behind every great magician lies not magic, but a scientific explanation and hours of disciplined work: developing, testing, reflecting, adjusting. While what they do may appear effortless – even spontaneous – it is anything but.

I first met John when he was taking up his role as Honorary Professor at the University of Exeter Business School. He was aware that people often labelled their interactions with him as having a sense of magic, or him having a magic quality. While he appreciated the compliment, he also found it intensely frustrating. John cares deeply for his own growth and those of others. He wanted to understand more clearly what he does and how he does it, for his own curiosity, and even more, to be able to share that knowledge if possible. That was the challenge he brought to me.

In contrast to a traditional magic circle – where magicians share tricks of their trade only with a select few to maintain the sense of mystery to their audience – John wants to share with everyone. He wants a world where anyone can learn how to become exceptional.

Drawing on principles of qualitative research methods, in particular a grounded theory approach, I observed John in different situations. I coded as many different aspects of his interactions as possible, identifying patterns and themes that emerged, not looking simply for repetition but for different examples of behaviours, language and emotions that expressed the same underlying ideas. We reflected together throughout the process, building understanding as the data amassed, and continued observations until we reached a point of saturation in the data where no new insights emerged.

As you might expect (and if you don't now, you will once you've finished reading the book), John didn't just want the overall end report. He wanted the entire database of coded examples that sat underneath the analysis – to dissect, digest and return to over time. He relishes that level of depth and rigour, and his commitment to reflection is part of what makes him so exceptional.

This piece of work with John is one I felt truly honoured to be involved in. It will always be one of my personal and professional highlights. It's a rare and remarkable leader who invites such a study – and does so with real curiosity, openness, ability and willingness to share their introspection. If you don't know already, yes: John is just as engaging, caring, perceptive and insightful in 'real life' as he appears wherever else you've encountered him. I share this because it feels important for you to know that the exercise of this book isn't about demonstrating his extraordinariness. Of all the people he could have asked, I think John invited me to write this foreword because I can offer a unique insight and verification. I know first-hand, the research, care, depth of thought, and authenticity with which John has written this book.

Sometimes we might want to enjoy the pretence of magic by not understanding how a trick was done. But there are times when understanding deepens the awe, when unpacking the detail only heightens the sense of wonder. That's what working with John felt like. Being let into his 'not magic' circle didn't ruin the effect for me; it continues to enhance it. And I trust it will for you too, as you immerse yourself in this book.

My work with John was a starting point – a framework behind this book – and I'm delighted to see that skeleton beneath what is now there. At the end of my report, I wrote that I looked forward to seeing what happened next. This book is what happened next. It's not magic – it's the ordinary turned exceptional. John offers leaders that same possibility: by breaking down what may look like magic into concrete and achievable steps, he shows how extraordinary outcomes come from consistent and deliberate practice of ordinary skills.

Make no mistake, John does not offer any quick fixes. Instead, through a series of insights and stories, complemented with detailed exercises to turn principles into practice, John offers you the scaffolding for deep development through conscious, sustained effort. Like a pianist practising scales with a metronome, he invites you to grow your leadership muscles through deliberate, sometimes painstaking, practice – and in doing so, choose to be exceptional.

In *It's Not Magic: Ordinary Skills for Exceptional Leaders*, John invites all of us — not a select few — into what would otherwise be his magic circle. He doesn't offer tricks, he offers practice. He makes himself open and vulnerable, laying out the habits, the principles, the mindset, the attention to detail and the care required to lead with consistent and positive impact. This book is full of prompts, tools, reflections, and provocations — all designed not just to show what John does, but to help you build your own practice.

And so, in this book you get two things (*at least*): first, an eye-opening insight into the behind-the-scenes effort and discipline it takes to make exceptional leadership look effortless. And second, a generous, practical guide to how you can do the same. John isn't trying to impress you — he's inviting you to begin, to engage, to practise and to lead with intention.

As ever, with John, *It's not Magic* comes with a provocation. Whether we choose to acknowledge it or not, we are all leaders to someone, formally or informally. As John says, we are all giants to someone. Our behaviour always has an impact on someone in some way. John urges us to be conscious in our effort to shape the impact we will inevitably have — whether deliberate or not — on others.

Whether or not you choose to apply what's offered in this book is both a choice and a responsibility. The beauty of what John has created here is that it's not magic. It's something better. It's something you can do. The invitation and tools are ready and waiting for you to begin when you turn the page – the choice is yours.

—Dr Michelle Mahdon

INTRODUCTION

IT'S NOT
MAGIC. . .
IT'S HUMAN

This being my third book, it's tempting to believe I don't need an introduction, but if you're new to me, I imagine there might be some essential credibility-building to do.

My official biography opines that I am a Chartered Psychologist and Associate Fellow of the British Psychological Society (BPS), a Professor of Leadership at the University of Exeter Business School, and a *New York Times* and *Sunday Times* bestselling author.

I am a Fellow and Chartered Scientist at the Institute of Science and Technology. I've served as a non-executive director on FTSE companies. I was a 10-year director of the UK's largest healthcare organisation, and I have since advised the boards of global public companies in industries including finance, law, technology, engineering, publishing, retail and more.

If social proof is important, I'm one of LinkedIn's Top Voices and recognised as a leading influencer in human resources (HR) and organisational culture. My previous book, *The Promises of Giants*, is a rallying cry for leaders to embrace authenticity, drive ethical change, and become forces for good in their organisations, without sacrificing commercial success. I'm pleased to say it continues to shape how leaders worldwide think about their impact and legacy.

A few years ago, I created a short paragraph to use as part of a speaking introduction, as there are usually visually impaired people in any audience. Like most accommodations designed for one group of people, I've found it handy to help most people see and hear me more accurately.

I am a Black man of mixed heritage, standing six feet eight inches (203 cm) tall, with a white beard that is usually neatly trimmed but has moments where it goes rogue. I move deliberately, minimising unnecessary movement despite and perhaps because of my stature. I use my hands expressively but sparingly, employing precise gestures to emphasise key points rather than broad or dramatic movements. I pause – a lot – to ensure my sentences are well constructed, to give people time to consider what I say, and a host of other reasons I will describe in some of the later chapters.

Most of all, I am a nerd, a geek and a giant. So nerdy, I have been anointed a Jedi by Mark Hamill himself! Who congratulated me for all my achievements and told everyone, 'The force is strong with this one'.

The origins of this book started more than a decade ago. I was visiting a private boarding school on the East Coast of America, famous for producing US presidents. My team and I had been called in to support them as they began to understand that their students might not have been effectively equipped for the demands of what we were then calling a 'VUCA' (Volatility, Uncertainty, Complexity and Ambiguity) world by their existing curriculum and methods of teaching.

We delivered a series of 'high-intensity days' where (almost) every hour of a day, from an early breakfast to dinners at night, would be dedicated to rolling interactions – a mixture of speaking, coaching and advisory sessions with select student leaders, faculty and parents. You might suspect this was in response to some well-publicised mis-step or problem. While that certainly was one of the reasons my team and I might be called in, many of these were schools trying to show initiative and get ahead of the challenges they saw on the horizon for their faculty, staff and students.

On one occasion, I was visiting two teachers later at night who were also 'house parents' – teachers who lived in the residences to ensure the younger children had supervision and support – and while talking to them as we wandered the hallways on their evening rounds, reflecting on the discussions we'd had earlier, a girl, perhaps 16 years old, appeared around a corner and asked if she could talk to me.

I obliged gladly, in part because it was clear she was distressed. I remember stooping to talk to her in hushed tones, turning my back, putting my body between her and her 'house parents' to manufacture some privacy.

As we spoke, she cried a little. For a child at home, close to her loving parents and surrounded by the familiar, I'm confident the problem she described wouldn't have manifested tears, but it felt overwhelming for her in this setting.

As we talked, I could hear the two teachers talking in hushed tones, watching and narrating this incredibly ordinary and intuitive interaction. As my conversation concluded, the girl asked if she could have a hug – and I said yes, hugged her, and before she could wander away to her room through the darkened hallways, I heard the two educators excitedly whisper, 'He's doing it'.

Even as you read this, you can recognise the unremarkable nature of the interaction. Most of you would and indeed have intuitively done the same thing, whether it's another parent's child lost in a shop or found fallen on a playground. We know what to do.

Please suspend your suspicion of the educators in question. I remember them as dedicated, if new, to their 'house parent' roles. But I was struck by their perception that anything 'magic' was happening in the interaction.

I get this a lot – I am asked by people who want to know how I do something they find challenging, and the answer feels underwhelmingly mundane. I can see the disappointment in people's faces as their expressions scream, 'Is that all?!'

And, yes, it is – small things in thoughtful combination, consistently and with intention. That's all it is. Little tiny points of light that together create something spectacular.

The point of this book is to present you with all the dull, ordinary, energy-expensive, but transformative behaviours and actions that make up qualities that we mistakenly believe to be innate or reserved for a few 'charismatic', 'persuasive' or 'influential' people with 'gravitas' or 'presence'.

This book owes a debt to the remarkable Dr Michelle Mahdon, a colleague from the University of Exeter Business School. Without her, I wouldn't have had the means to begin to describe what I know and have learned from others, and all too often take for granted. I would have written a book, but not one with equal utility or so opportune for these challenging times, where exceptional leadership role models exist but seem overwhelmed by exceptionally prevalent bad examples.

A couple of years ago, I encountered a problem in my team, where my success with clients – my ability to manage challenging interactions and work with diverse people and organisations from wildly different sectors – seemed to be stupefying my peers. Even when I spoke to students at Exeter, many capable and skilled graduate students seemed to think of themselves as almost genetically underequipped, incapable of my 'rare' skills. Skills they more often attributed to people entirely different from them – in fact, to anyone except themselves.

I approached Michelle, and being the outstanding scientist she is, she suggested we tackle this methodologically and do a study to see if she could determine what I was doing when I was 'doing it'.

I told Michelle I knew I wasn't magic. I needed my team and, indeed, the leaders I advise, coach, support and challenge every day to understand this, lest it become an excuse to lower their leadership ambition or ignore the expectations placed on them by their teams, clients and all those who look up to them.

So, we embarked on a surreal study of one.

I was observed in university lectures, larger corporate presentations, client advisory conversations, and one-to-one coaching interactions. She spoke to my APS Intelligence colleagues and discussed my perspectives on my style, approach and techniques with me.

It was a strange experience to consider myself deeply introspective and yet find that while I had some answers to 'why' I did what I did in my more 'therapeutic' or educational interactions with others, I had less access than I'd imagined to 'how' I got the intended results from those interactions.

I found the process of this study chastening if educational, but the results themselves were deeply challenging. When I saw the summary document, just five pages and 1,835 words, I was shaken – I got the results I wanted.

And I hated them.

Along with this revelation, I clearly saw that what I did wasn't magic, and perhaps for the first time, I understood how important it had become to me, even without my conscious noticing, that I was *seen* to be somehow imbued with mysterious Jedi magic.

Don't get me wrong. I had expected that some combination of more basic skills would contribute most of what made me effective as a speaker, coach and indeed a psychologist but I had hoped that some small percentage, perhaps just 2%, would have been impossible, even for an intellect like Michelle's, to define; but equally so notable, that this undefined and unique ingredient would need to be drawn out and written in the research as 'an enigmatic mystery worthy of future study'.

No such luck.

As it turns out, I don't have 'a very particular set of skills' after all. I have an array of extraordinarily ordinary skills, techniques and otherwise utterly obtainable knowledge that I use, at best, in interesting but far from unique combinations. Combinations that anyone with some time, conviction and tenacity can garner and expect similar results.

At the same time, I realised I was guilty of gatekeeping this knowledge. I think, at first, I did this in service of not insulting people who so effusively compliment me after interactions they find hard to fathom, but later I know I must have continued because the aura of magic that this approach cultivated – to no one's benefit but my own – became intoxicating.

The result of this is that some of you reading this, who've met me, heard me speak in person or watched one of my numerous videos on social media, are already creating reasons why you 'could never do X as well as I do' or shaking your head reflecting on something you think I do with ease that could never be your second-nature skill.

I can only apologise for my part and tell you this book is for you. And while not everything I describe in this book will become easy for you, you can learn, adapt and grow with every element I describe in the following chapters.

My mother once told me that the most unlikely of people, in the most improbable of circumstances, can become extraordinary, and I believed her. But like a depth charge sinking silently into my consciousness for years before exploding, I now think I finally understand what she meant.

She didn't mean for me to believe that I would contain enigmatic, unknowable 'stuff' that made me unique, but rather that each of us need only to embrace the limitless supply of ordinary ingredients that, with effort, will, intention and a little creativity, can create recipes that can feel to each person we meet like they were made only and especially for them.

There will be questions about authenticity to address throughout this book. You might be concerned that some people may grab a sentence or tool from a random chapter to bamboozle people they hope to exploit.

Sadly, these people exist, always looking for shortcuts to influence and impact.

Still, I take solace in knowing that every detail I describe here will be impotent without the required mindset and intention, not to mention their consistent use in thoughtful combination. Anyone who thinks this book is a guide that can be mined for misuse will appear no less than a stereotypical used-car salesman to those they'd hope to manipulate.

Everyone can tell the difference between someone who asks, 'How are you?' with their body language and tone oozing the expectation of a genuine response that they'll willingly stop to hear versus those who use the exact words but convey explicitly that they want you to say the word 'fine' in response, even as they've walked indifferently out of earshot.

Thinking there are shortcuts to influence, leadership effectiveness and the motivation of other human beings is indeed a path to the dark side, and anyone doing this will be quickly exposed. Being exposed doesn't mean you can't find a group of people to exploit. We can see those so-called 'leaders' out there in force, but I have a sense that those figures aren't buying or reading my book. More's the pity.

I invite you to embrace the simple but energy-expensive tools and activities in this book, which will support you in becoming the kind of leader others will find engaging, compelling and worthwhile to emulate and follow.

Our political, business and academic landscape is littered with prominent people who appear to have modelled their leadership approach from the playground bully playbook. These people vigorously defend their right never to advance or improve those childish approaches while seemingly escaping sanction for their bad choices.

We need glimmers of light in this world to act as role models, rational oases and reliable sources of resilience; even when such people aren't nearby, they – you – provide a tangible sense of hope like a distant promise of a more humane experience. Human history is littered with apocryphal stories of someone caring to do the hard work of leadership, thereby changing someone's life forever.

Part of my goal with *It's Not Magic* is to help you realise that those stories don't have to be rare, distant and as incandescent as the sun to be profound; they can be ordinary and frequent – and be all the more awe-inspiring for it.

I celebrated New Year 2025 from the roof terrace of my new flat in East London. Twenty-two floors up with panoramic views, my friends and I jostled for the best positions to see the 'official' New Year fireworks over the London Eye.

3... 2... 1... Happy New Year – the official fireworks over The Eye went off, and that was the last moment I watched them because, suddenly, from every angle, there was light. We scattered, jumping on chairs and tables this time with space aplenty as the view was... everywhere. I have had the privilege of many breathtaking experiences in my life, but I will never forget this. Sparks of light across the horizon, close to and far – pulsing like the infrastructure of London itself was alive. The closer fireworks illuminated flats nearby that, in four months of living in this flat, I'd never noticed, and for the first time, distant neighbours caught each other's eye, smiling and waving from windows and balconies.

I only realised the official fireworks were over when the BBC coverage we were listening to in the background announced it; we were still entranced by the impact of the best example I can imagine of tiny sparks of light capturing the moment better than any lone big show.

From Croyden to Enfield, Hillingdon to Havering, one Roman Candle from a back garden, rogue bottle rocket from a car park, and I'm certain, even as I didn't see it, a solitary sparkler flourished enthusiastically from a Juliet balcony, combined to move me in a way that I could not have anticipated. But in a way that strengthened my resolve for the year ahead.

As I write this, it's the 2 January 2025. This moment has such undeniable gravity that my mind orbits it, and with every elliptical pass, I am grateful and re-energised.

I am 54 years old. I've known that people set off fireworks at New Year for a *long* time, but even as I've known it, it's been impossible for me to imagine what I saw on 1 January 2025 or anticipate the impact of witnessing all those sparks of light.

We see too few examples of leadership in the minutiae, small expressions of people fulfilling their leadership promise from whatever space they have. Here is our opportunity to add to a glorious cacophony.

If you're interested, you can see a snippet of video from that night on my Twitter timeline[1] (if Twitter, or X, as its mercurial owner renamed it, still exists as you read this!).

So this is my ask: Be a spark of light – a little more enduring and eco-friendly than fireworks, perhaps – because someone out there needs to see you glowing on the horizon. With that commitment from everyone reading this book, we can create a collective that builds hope, enables resilience, and encourages everyone else to shine a little brighter.

If I do my job right here, a creeping sense of disappointment will hit on two fronts. One, when you continue reading elements, actions and approaches that are, in isolation, the most common of common sense and the revelation I experienced at receiving my personal research report – that I should have been able to figure this out on my own – will come crashing over you.

The second hit comes when your mind matches some of these common-sense solutions with recent or distant memories of moments when you could have deployed them to create better outcomes for yourself or others.

I implore you not to punish yourself. We are linear creatures, burdened with a selective memory of the past that all too often appears committed to wounding us. But ahead is what matters, even where the opportunity to make amends for past misdeeds is concerned.

So, forward and onwards, with all this 'stuff', we should have known but didn't.

The test of us as leaders isn't in how deeply and publicly we lament our past missteps, mourning what we've done in the past and can't change, but whether we choose to consistently and conscientiously deploy new leadership discoveries, piece by piece, spark by spark until the space around us is alive with light.

Fundamentally, leading effectively and being seen as a 'luminous' leader that people want to follow requires a willingness to consistently and continuously exert energy and acquire skills.

The reason we have so few laudable leaders – and fundamentally why so few people *want* to be great leaders – is not the rarity of their skills or the ultimate responsibility of their office; it's the daily mundanity of acquiring essential qualities and the ongoing effort to apply them consistently.

In my travels, I have met many people who say they desire the title of leader; for some, it's their whole point for working, their *raison d'être*. Inevitably, however, they realise that leading well is energy-intensive, above and beyond any technical requirements. In my opinion, this is why so few people become great leaders: They love the idea of the title but don't like the weight of the crown.

ORGANISATION OF THE BOOK

This book is structured in three parts. Part I focuses on building the foundations of effective leadership – internal disciplines such as commitment, authentic presence and perceptive listening. Part II turns those foundations outward, exploring how to communicate with intention, empower others and evolve under pressure. Part III expands your leadership influence further, helping you adapt to complexity, grow others and enrich your credibility across time and through complex challenges.

Each part builds on the last. There are many practical elements, but they won't manifest just by reading – they will require attention, reflection and effort.

Leadership is not bestowed. It is not a product of 'charisma' or title. It is earned through daily deliberate actions, intentional choices and a refusal to default to convenience over conviction.

Unsurprisingly, this book offers no magic, only the ordinary skills that, when applied with consistency and care, make extraordinary leadership possible.

What you choose to do with these skills will define the kind of leader – and person – you will become.

PART I

BUILDING THE FOUNDATIONS

CHAPTER ONE

UNLOCKING YOUR POTENTIAL AND TURNING PRINCIPLES INTO PRACTICE

IT'S NOT MAGIC. . . IT'S A COMMITMENT

Each of the chapters of this book will include a section called 'Principles into Practice: Making it Real' that will include one or more of the following elements:

- *Scripts:* Structured formats with verbatim sections for navigating specific conversations and scenarios.
- *Tools:* Frameworks and checklists to guide decision-making and interaction in various leadership contexts.
- *Activities:* Hands-on exercises, reflections and assignments to apply and reinforce leadership concepts.
- *Commitments:* Actionable pledges to reinforce learning and encourage personal accountability.

Not every chapter will have all these elements, but each chapter will ask for at least one commitment and another aspect to explore, such as taking what you're reading, combining it with what you're thinking, and making it real.

This section is designed to unlock your potential by taking what you already know and what you are inspired to consider when reading this book to create and execute your own blueprint. Instead of having a story or concept to smile or reminisce over 12 months from now, I want tangible change to show for it.

It's worth outlining each of the elements in more detail, in part because it is the teaching approach I take especially in workplaces.

SCRIPTS

Scripts are structured, pre-planned conversational blueprints designed to guide specific types of dialogue with clarity and purpose. They include verbatim phrases or prompts to ensure the intent of the conversation is communicated effectively and consistently. Scripts serve as a scaffold for complex or emotionally charged discussions, offering leaders a tested pathway to navigate challenging interactions while focusing on the desired outcomes. They provide a foundation for confidence, clarity and skilful delivery. Importantly, scripts are adaptable and re-purposeful. With experience, you will find ways to add your own wrinkles to a script to make them more you without losing any effectiveness. In addition, you will notice that with some simple modifications, scripts designed for one purpose can bring fantastic benefits in other contexts.

TOOLS

Tools are adaptable frameworks or structured guides designed to help leaders approach specific interactions or decisions with greater precision and insight, usually without prescribing exact wording. These may include checklists, step-by-step progressions, or strategic frameworks that outline considerations and best practices to follow. They also include simple behavioural techniques that enhance your ability to operate effectively. Tools are crafted to simplify complex processes, prevent common missteps, and enhance the effectiveness of decision-making or communication. They empower leaders to achieve consistency and impact while fostering personal and organisational growth.

ACTIVITIES

Activities are experiential learning tasks that deepen understanding and drive reflection on key concepts. They can be thought-provoking questions, reflective journaling prompts, actionable exercises, or curated resources such as recommended readings or videos. Activities encourage leaders to apply insights to their unique contexts, engage in meaningful dialogue, or explore new perspectives through practice. These tasks are designed to build self-awareness, develop skills, and foster connection with others, embedding learning into everyday practice.

COMMITMENTS

Commitments offer a practical way to translate learning into meaningful action. Each chapter concludes with a discrete, manageable, yet stretching challenge that aligns with the chapter's themes. These commitment requests can be a simple sentence asking you to pick something from the chapter and deliver on the action or apply the learning. Don't mistake the simplicity of the request with comfort in making the commitment. These commitments inspire immediate action and longer-term growth, helping you solidify the insights they've gained.

Commitments can be divided into two types:

- *Process commitments* focus on how something is done, encouraging behavioural shifts, habit formation or refined approaches to recurring tasks or interactions.
- *Outcome commitments* aim for measurable or noticeable results, driving the reader towards goals or tangible endpoints reflecting real change.

By incorporating both types of commitments, you can develop a well-rounded approach to personal development, addressing both day-to-day behaviours and tangible building blocks for longer-term aspirations.

I encourage you to set clear deadlines for each commitment, whether to achieve a specific result or embed a new habit into your routine. By engaging with these challenges, you'll take ownership of your development, ensuring the concepts from each chapter move beyond reflection into purposeful, sustained change. You are not limited to one commitment per chapter, but it's better to complete one commitment for each chapter than find yourself with tens of incomplete commitments hanging over you as you read on. By all means, be zealous in your appetite for change and growth, but be pragmatic and kind in your approach.

Before we go any further, we will consider how we create a commitment. Without meaning to patronise, we often assume this is obvious and embedded. After all, most of us have tasks to complete and people who rely on us to do 'stuff' at home and work, so we've all got this, right?

In case you'd like a refresher, there's a science to making effective commitments. I want you to consider the following 'Tool' as a foundation for bringing about the effective personal and professional changes you want.

TOOL: THE KEY ELEMENTS OF EFFECTIVE COMMITMENTS

There are 13 key elements for making effective commitments:

1. Specificity and Clarity
   - Define your commitment precisely, detailing your actions, when and how. For example, instead of committing to 'exercising more', pick an activity type, duration and number of days a week you plan to do the activity.
   - Your commitment may require other actions. For example, I get up early, about 05:30, not for those ridiculous reasons some random 'alpha man' suggests but because I love to ride my bike. However, I don't love riding my bike in London at rush hour – so I get up early to facilitate my commitment to bike riding (and safety!)
2. Achievability and Incrementality
   - As you set your mind on a commitment, you will find precursor actions, some of which are chunky enough to be commitments in their own right. Don't be afraid to separate them out and make them precursor commitments.

From my previous example, I might have committed to getting up earlier for two weeks before I followed up by getting up and getting on my bike for my first ride.

- Don't try to 'eat the elephant'. Break up larger goals into smaller, but still challenging and meaningful, chunks.
- Don't commit to someone else's version of you. However simple or easy to achieve, making commitments based on someone else's expectations or demands of you, especially absent any personal stake based on who you are and what you really want to achieve in the future, will either fail to happen or in success, feel hollow.

3. Personal Relevance
   - Meaningfulness is important – while achieving a goal that isn't meaningful to you is possible, it's often more onerous and injurious in the process. You don't need to commit to doing something for the same reasons as others, but whatever reason you choose must speak – at least – to you. Find that reason, embrace it, and don't worry whether it 'resonates' with others as long as it compels you.
   - Ensure commitments align with your values and longer-term aspirations. This might mean really considering your longer-term aspirations if you haven't already!
   - Engage in personal reflection on the ongoing relevance of any commitment over time. Is it still serving you? Is it still congruent with your values and aspirations?

4. Public and Written Nature
   - Written (and especially handwritten)[1] commitments make for stronger, more enduring behaviour change. So, whether you are a classic 'pen and moleskine notebook' person or, like me, for organisational purposes alone, you've shifted to Goodnotes or similar, I encourage you to write down, date and time stamp your commitments.

9

- The literature encourages public commitments to increase accountability[2] where commitments are concerned. It seems to me that this is more effective when the people you share your commitment with both care about you and you care what they think about you. Banging off a commitment tweet on Twitter (it will always be referred to as Twitter) to a mass of faceless followers will likely be less effective than curating an audience that will care about your declaration and want to be a part of your achieving it.

5. Voluntary Participation
   - I will make some suggestions about the nature and scope of commitments you might make, but I must allow you to choose your specific commitments freely. Otherwise, I risk dampening your intrinsic motivation[3] and violating any number of these guidelines by making your commitment my commitment.

6. Positive Framing
   - Frame commitments in terms of positive actions rather than restrictions.[4] The way I speak and write often focuses on what something isn't before I describe what something is – this is a rhetorical habit rather than a reflection of my optimism or pessimism. However, where commitments are concerned, it is helpful to frame as much as possible, to present them as actions to embrace rather than restrictions to avoid. So it's not that you will 'not eat Nutella for every meal', but rather you 'will ensure that one meal per day con tains green vegetables and a source of protein'.

7. Accountability Mechanisms
   - Use tools like trackers or visual aids to monitor and display progress. This doesn't mean you must create a personal dashboard, but you will need to understand how you are

doing against your commitments. Some tracking will help you stay engaged, adjust your efforts and experience a sense of accomplishment as you progress against your commitment.[5]

- Sometimes, behavioural contracts that clearly outline responsibilities and consequences can be useful.[6] You might already be doing this with little 'deals' you do with yourself – 'If I eat a healthy breakfast and lunch, I can have a small slice of cheesecake with dinner!' or 'If I write another 5,000 words this afternoon, I can get a Chinese meal as a reward' or 'If I don't finish my homework by 6pm, I can't go to the party'.

- Accountability partners – find someone who is also questing for something important (it doesn't need to be the same thing as you) to hold you accountable for your commitment. Bear in mind these are most powerful when reciprocal – when you are bound to monitor, support and challenge them to achieve their stated goals, as they are yours.

8. Social Support
   - Find groups of people with similar sets of goals and embrace peer support networks to encourage follow-through. One such way is to join the LinkedIn group 'Find Your Giant Community', where you will find a diverse and wonderfully committed group of leaders and aspiring leaders from across the world and across sectors, ready to connect and support you.

   - Some of you will be part of professional networks with some utility. For me, there are networks for the British Psychological Society (BPS), the Association for Business Psychologists (ABP), the Chartered Institute for Personnel and Development (CIPD) and the Institute of Science and Technology (IST) that I find most supportive in my growth journey. However, I'm aware that not all of you will have networks that are so interested or engaged in your personal and professional growth. Find a network that will work for you.

9. Feedback and Evaluation
   - From the moment you write your commitment, provide yourself with regular opportunities for self-reflection and progress assessment. I tend to do this by scheduling time in my diary to reflect on my success toward my goals.
   - If you've engaged accountability buddies or have people close to you at work or home who are on their own development journey, offer and request mutual feedback sessions to review progress, adjust commitments, celebrate milestones and adjust goals as needed.

10. Intrinsic Motivation Focus
    - Connect commitments with personal values and long-term aspirations. Everyone needs a 'why'. If it's hidden or unspoken, if it's euphemistic or a lie, your chances of engaging your intrinsic motivational resources are limited. Name your truth – be explicit and direct about why you want to do something. Even if that truth is 'I want to stick two fingers up to [insert name of the bad boss here]', that reality is going to engage your motivation more than something generic that's been mentally photoshopped for public acceptability, like 'I just want to help people'.
    - There are techniques for personal compassion and motivation aligned with the practice of 'motivational interviewing' that could be useful to consider to maintain your

momentum. I discuss them in Chapter 6 in the context of helping colleagues and friends transform perceived weaknesses. When you get to that chapter, I will remind you that these techniques, supposedly for those we wish to lead or influence, can also be effectively deployed to support our own ambitions.

11. Tangibility and Noticeability

I'm a psychologist – I am fascinated by mindset and the mind – even now, I want to spin off a soliloquy about how little we understand about the mind, the mind/body paradox and, as I will discuss later in Chapter 4, how not all the voices in your head are you! Until then, remember that your commitments are enhanced when you:

- Focus on observable behaviours and actions rather than abstract concepts.
- Ensure commitments are noticeable, even when not measurable, so they can be easily sensed if not monitored by you and others.

For example, 'I will demonstrate my gratitude by thanking colleagues in specific ways related to a tangible contribution they make' is leagues ahead of 'I won't take my team for granted' as a commitment.

12. Time-Bound Nature

- Set clear timeframes for commitments to create urgency and facilitate evaluation. Remember 'What by when' as a mantra – you will achieve this specific outcome or habitual practice by a certain and specific date.
- Create an interim check-in point if an outcome or target date is over three weeks away.

13. Flexibility and Adaptability
    - Allow for adjustments to commitments based on progress and changing circumstances. You are legitimately busy people with pulls on your time, drains to your energy and, for some of us, fires to fight on multiple fronts. In addition, we exist in a world of change and novel and unexpected events.
    - The check-in points for your medium- to longer-term goals must incorporate amendment and reprioritisation of goals and targets.
    - Avoid adaptations or extensions based on whim, frivolous desires or trivial distractions.
    - Do not punish yourself for the adaptations you make or the extensions you allow yourself when they are borne of a tactical or strategic necessity.

Commitments are catalysts for personal and professional growth. They are the cornerstone of personal development, serving as discrete, manageable, yet challenging goals that readers set for themselves after completing each chapter. These commitments are designed to be both achievable and stretching, encouraging readers to push beyond their comfort zones and make tangible progress towards their goals.

Each chapter of this book introduces a new commitment, either building upon the previous ones or challenging ever-further change, to create a comprehensive framework for personal growth. I encourage you to set specific deadlines for completing or habituating each commitment, ensuring accountability and measurable progress. Don't forget; you don't have to do this alone – you aren't the only one reading this book or seeking ways to improve their leadership – there are online fora, IRL group meetings, book clubs and other methods to find people to share your successes and anxieties on this journey. In my last book, *The Promises of Giants*, I encouraged you to create a 'Cabinet' of people to support and advise you. In this ever-fractured world, that still stands as good advice, but perhaps more than ever, we need to see more than a group we are familiar with to an inspiring Tribe of people, different in their own ways and bound not by politics or nationalism, but in their desire to become the leaders their communities, teams and organisations deserve.

Principles into Practice: Making it Real

Using the commitment framework, make a commitment about how you will read this book. You've got other priorities and demands on your time, so be practical, but:

1. How often, when and for how long will you carve out time to read this book?
2. With whom will you share your thoughts and reflections, and how often?
3. Pick one personally important person to share your commitment and ask them to check in with you on your success regularly (perhaps monthly?) (This may or may not be the same person with whom you share your reflections.

If you are reading this book and don't know anyone else doing the same, write down your commitment, following the commitment guidance.

(Continued)

Find a new notebook or digital folder to collect all your commitments, reflections and questions. If you have a physical copy of this book, feel free to write all over it and add Post-it notes as an alternative.

Good evidence shows that handwriting notes, reflections and commitments are more effective for memory and actually keeping commitments over time versus typing or just mulling your thoughts in your head.

While typing may be faster and more convenient in some situations, the evidence suggests that handwriting (whether digital or 'real')[7] offers significant learning and memory benefits and personal goal-setting and commitment. Handwriting goals and plans may increase the likelihood of remembering and achieving them.

If you are part of a group or you know another person reading this book, you are going to do a 'digital pair and share' exercise with them:

1. Write your commitment.
2. Share your commitment with a partner who will check it to ensure the commitment guidance has been followed.
3. Once checked, one person in a pair gets both phones with the photo app open and on the 'video' setting.
4. They point both cameras at the other person, and when the other person is ready, they begin to record.
5. When recording has begun, they speak their commitment.

6. Both phones are swapped, and the process is repeated for the second person.

7. You now both have a copy of your own and the other person's commitment on your phones.

8. Mark these videos as "favourites" so that you can access them easily, and they will pop up as reminders occasionally.

This process can also be done on Teams, Zoom or another virtual messaging platform. The key is ensuring you both have a recording that encapsulates both commitments and that you set reminders to look them up on occasion so you can check your growth against your goals.

CHAPTER TWO

THE POWER OF AUTHENTIC PRESENCE

IT'S NOT MAGIC. . . IT'S MINDSET

I received a wonderful comment on social media recently. I had appeared on my friend Dan LeBatard's Radio Show in the United States, speaking stridently against those who are cruel, bullying and otherwise act with disregard for others.

A listener commented: 'I like how he calls out bad behaviour so calmly; years of practice, I guess, and something I hope to keep getting better at.' Even as I told her that years of practice had built my skills and accelerated my balding head and greying beard, she replied, 'You do challenge with style and grace, and it's something I aspire to.'

I loved the compliment almost as much as I loved that she is already working to continue improving her authentic presence.

This chapter is not just about keeping cool in challenging circumstances; it's about creating a steady state for yourself that is present, controlled, appropriately focused and measured. It isn't just an external veneer; it's an internal state. Don't get me wrong, being able to tame your external emotional expression can come in handy, but to create an authentic leadership presence, more is required than that.

Presence has several nebulous definitions in the literature and customised definitions depending on the sector, industry or region in which you live. However, most of us recognise it in others and can see how they'd benefit from having more of it. Regardless of the definitions, it's still essential for people interested in shaping organisational, community or societal culture, enhancing team engagement and cohesion and driving and sustaining high-performance cultures.

Among the various definitions, 'having a presence' usually refers to a leader's ability to project self-assurance, competence and authenticity in interactions and decision-making processes. It encompasses physical and psychological aspects of a leader's demeanour and impact on others.

Before we dive in, there is an elephant in this room I'd like to discuss.

Many, if not most, of the 'broad brush' traits such as 'presence' or 'influence' are traditionally masculine-designated. Even when women, non-binary or non-traditionally masculine men have it, we inevitably see it devalued and called something else, something less recognisably important.

We know that positive attributes for one type of person (typically men) can transmogrify when possessed by another identity. 'Assertiveness' becomes 'pushy' or 'aggressive', 'influence' becomes 'manipulation' or 'conniving', and 'presence' can become 'intimidating' or 'attention-seeking'.

All of us reading this – and as a man saying this – have to be constantly vigilant of this temptation to attribute gender and other identities to powerful leadership traits and, as such, to distort those traits when not possessed by the people we might stereotypically expect.

If you're a man reading this, especially one of those seen as a more 'typical man' in your context, you'll need to remain vigilant while using these techniques and educate those still stuck in those old patterns of 'identity-locked' thinking.

When contemplating presence, I want you to consider two different but related definitions.

The first is 'being present', a term most often used to describe the intentional and authentic state of being fully engaged in the current moment. This state is characterised by focused attention, openness and multidimensional (physical, emotional, cognitive) vigilance and receptivity to oneself and others. It involves bringing all of yourself to an encounter with others while simultaneously creating a space for genuine curiosity, connection and understanding based on what someone else is bringing.

The second is 'having (a compelling) presence', an expression used to describe the nebulous but palpable factors that make a person stand out without trying. They often refer to a combination of subtle qualities that create a powerful impression. This type of presence is less about deliberate actions and more about an authentic way of being that naturally draws attention and respect.

For brevity, I will talk about the factors consistent with both types of presence. Some will be more relevant for 'having presence' than 'being present', but there is some overlap because many of the precursor factors are the same, even as their presentation may differ in each context.

As I highlight strategies for developing a powerful yet approachable presence, you will see how self-awareness, self-assurance, proactive attentiveness, precise language, vigilance to body language and tonal cues, and the ability to blot out distractions help you too.

SELF-AWARENESS

Most people don't know themselves very well at all.

When we think of school-age children growing up, the syllabi they experience at school, the methods of examination (in the United Kingdom and most similar systems at least), and indeed the questions we hear visiting relatives ask, all steer the conversation towards 'what will you do when you grow up?' Ironically, this approach is, for the most part, as useless for helping a person select their career as it is responsible for discouraging introspection. I can't imagine who truly believes that most of the jobs we're asking a 15-year-old in 2025 to select as their vocation will reliably exist when they're 25. Regardless, many of us choose arbitrary academic subjects, academic and vocational qualifications and career pathways in pursuit of an answer to that question of what we will do.

Many of us still spend our whole lives thinking about what we will do under the constant pressure of role changes and organisational 'transformation', so perhaps it should be no surprise that while striving to answer the question of what we will do (for a living), we didn't spend enough, if any, time considering who we are or will become.

I am a big fan of Dr Tasha Eurich's work on self-awareness.[1] She's probably too polite to call herself a guru of self-awareness, but she speaks and writes in a way that all of us mere mortals can understand.

She has done studies and discovered that 95% of people believe they are self-aware. The punchline, of course, is that when she probed them, she found only 10–15% truly were. The first challenge of self-awareness is in the numbers – most people think they know themselves better than they do.

This has challenges for being seen as having a compelling presence and for people to believe you are fully present with them.

It is nearly impossible to present yourself genuinely if what you are presenting is a guess, an approximation, or, all too often, a hopeful aspiration of a future or ideal self. You will leave people meeting you confused, as the 'you' you present to them falls further away from the 'you' they observe.

As a humanistic psychologist, by training, I was taught that incongruence is a source of internal distress and anxiety and, when observed by others, distrust and disquiet.

The incongruence of not understanding who you are in a given context is challenging for children. We can see the uncertainty in their faces and hear it in their plaintive questions as they seek to understand themselves and their world. So you can imagine, with some compassion, I hope, the fear such a revelation might cause someone otherwise accomplished and previously oblivious to their internal myopia.

This doesn't excuse the fact that a lack of self-awareness in influential people invariably causes harm to those they lead or have dominion over, but you can see why even and perhaps especially accomplished people find it hard to begin this challenge.

Dr Eurich[2] found that the more senior people become in organisations or systems, the less self-aware they tend to become and the worse they become at judging their levels of self-awareness. The very people at most risk of causing harm by their lack of self-awareness are most likely to have low self-awareness and not realise it.

Self-awareness is an essential precursor to presence because it grants you access to your values and beliefs and, over time, the ability to articulate them effectively and non-judgmentally in conversation with others. This clarity feels to others like reassuring transparency, even when their values and beliefs differ or even clash.

Equally, as people observe you *in situ* – at work or in another setting – an obvious alignment between your internal state and your external behaviour creates a reassuring resonance. Part of having a presence is the fact that 'what you see is what you get', a type of behavioural integrity that reassures people and makes you predictable in the best possible way.

Additionally, being present with others is often hampered by internal noise in response to external stimuli. One source of that noise is emotional triggers – your responses to interactions with people and contexts that introduce elements that set off a rapid, often emotional cascade in your head.

The more unaware you are of your propensity for being triggered in a particular situation or context, the more likely you will be pulled out of the moment because this undiscovered emotional charge internally ambushed you.

In the practical activities at the end of the chapter, we will explore specific techniques for managing emotional triggers and filling self-awareness blind spots.

One of my mentors in grad school was a working forensic psychologist. I remember practising a presentation on confidence in front of a small grad seminar group. I knew a lot about confidence because I played sports for a while and knew that confidence was a key to performance.

Early in grad school, I thought I knew much more than I actually understood.

I pontificated for a while, and when I was done, I got a warm reception and some useful feedback, but nothing to pull too hard on the strings of my argument about the directly proportional relationship between confidence and performance.

My mentor, however, took me aside at the end – I will always be grateful she did this one-on-one – and disassembled my thesis.

She worked with criminals and people with significant psychopathies and always noted that confidence was invariably one of the qualities they possessed in abundance.

This helped me understand the flaws in how we think about confidence broadly; it doesn't have a perfect positive correlation with the most important things conducive to effective, contemporary leadership and teaming. Even where performance, productivity, creativity, innovation, and the like are concerned, they appear to improve with increasing confidence, but that rise plateaus surprisingly early and then crashes dramatically.

A study completed in 2020 describes this 'Inverted U-shaped relationship' in the Yerkes-Dodson Law,[3] indicating something that you may have already intuitively divined: too much confidence is not only counterproductive but repellent. It lowers effectiveness in important individual and team characteristics and is a barrier to wanting to be close to that individual. That's the opposite of having presence.

On a purely anecdotal level, there isn't even one person reading this who doesn't know or hasn't observed someone in their orbit who would be so much better, more capable or more well-received if they were slightly less self-confident!

People perceived to have presence have self-assurance. This is a holistic belief in one's tenacity, skills and capabilities. Unlike confidence, which is often domain-specific ('I am great at parallel parking but bad at motorway driving at night'), self-assurance is characterised by a sense of accurate and objective understanding and inner trust in one's abilities, characteristics and skills. It means you have a sense of your capacity to handle various, even novel or unique, situations and challenges based on your clarity of insight rather than because you've seen or mastered a specific challenge before.

Self-assurance is an internal state of mind that allows individuals to approach tasks, decisions, and interactions with certainty and poise, regardless of external circumstances or prior experience. Although this is not always true, the sense you get from people that they can lead you to success despite not having done that task before is borne of your clear perception of their self-assurance.

What I have noted in the remarkable diversity of people I have coached and mentored over the years, or worked with as part of one of my teams' in-house programmes, is the lack of self-assurance present in highly competent and accomplished people.

When I ask people to talk about their 'areas for development' or their gaps in expertise, the list rolls off their tongue. Detailed and caustic as if, as they said it, they held no love for themselves at all.

Self-assurance is a commitment to an accelerated understanding of your assets. Many of you might counsel another that spending money if they don't know they have enough in their bank is irresponsible. Well, operating in the world without a clear understanding of your assets is similarly irresponsible and will cause you pain.

At the end of this chapter, we will engage in a practical exercise to help reveal and reinforce your self-assurance.

ENGAGED (AND ENGAGING) AWARENESS

I marvel at the ability of primary (elementary in the USA) school teachers to give their undivided attention to one person while still being aware of a group.

It's a skill for sure, but one you can learn. Engaged and engaging awareness, however, isn't just about being able to focus and switch focus on demand from person to person; it adds empathy and social awareness so you connect authentically with others' thoughts and feelings. In this context, your presence becomes a partnership with them rather than making them feel like objects in your personal petri dish.

I sat at breakfast in a Holiday Inn in Long Beach, California, a lifetime ago. By then, I'd been in the United States for a few years at college but hadn't made my NBA debut yet.

That being said, I had Americanised a little, and I sat in shorts, a sleeveless shirt, tube socks and slides as I ate my mountain of buffet eggs, pancakes and bacon indiscriminately drizzled in maple syrup. I was trying to ignore an older couple across the room as they whispered to each other and stared at me.

My every bite was scrutinised. I was irritated, but as ever, I wanted to avoid an energy-expensive interaction. Indeed, I was so desperate to ignore their incessant focus that I picked up a discarded *US Today* to distract me – that's always a sign of true desperation!

Suddenly, back in the real world, I was interrupted by the beaming couple standing next to me. They gratefully shared in an accent that was definitely not Californian (nor British), 'We just wanted to tell you it was a pleasure to watch you eat this morning!' Without waiting for a response, I watched them open-mouthed, as they shuffled away to do whatever tourists did in Long Beach 30 years ago.

Being present isn't just observational focus; it's scooping people up in your attention and helping them understand that your attention is in service of something mutual, more than just personal satisfaction or morbid curiosity.

It's not about whether that old couple who'd never seen a person eat breakfast with a knife and fork meant harm, but had clearly never considered whether their focus would negatively impact me.

I am mindful not to repeat what I have already written, so you can find more on this engaged awareness aspect of being present and the 'Passenger On Board' technique in Chapter 10 of *The Promises of Giants*.

Intention matters in presence. How do you want people to feel during and especially after interacting with you? Is it frightened? (I'm afraid too many leaders think their colleagues should shudder – just a little – in their presence.) Is it galvanised? Curious? Inspired?

There's a question I ask every client I work with. It's on a document we call a CCB ('confidential client briefing'), and it simply asks: 'What do you want your people to walk away thinking and feeling?'

Clients new to APS Intelligence often wonder why we ask this, but the answer is key to setting my intention, crafting my tone, and maintaining it. This question is a simple way to enhance your engagement with any audience of any size, and you might use it yourself to see the difference it makes.

You'll find a commitment exercise linked to this intention-setting later in the practical activities section.

SUBTLE BODY LANGUAGE CUES

Presence is often communicated through body language that is simultaneously relaxed and poised. Never so comfortable that you risk looking like former MP, Jacob Rees-Mogg, slumped in a soporific stupor on the benches of the House of Commons[4] as he did in 2019, and yet not rigid or obviously stressed either.

When I trained in Scottsdale in the offseason, my trainer, Warren, used to constantly reinforce to new participants in our sessions who tensed every muscle fibre as they attempted the agility and speed tests that they could never be fast that way: 'A relaxed body is an agile body'. I've never forgotten that advice, and it informs my public demeanour because I'm certain it applies as much to minds as it does to bodies.

I have witnessed the impression a person makes when at that sweet spot of relaxed readiness – a place where they are at pains to acknowledge obvious tensions and concerns in a given context yet simultaneously exude an assurance that they can handle whatever occurs. This is so clearly responsible for some of the comfort people take in that type of leader's company that we must explore some of its constituent parts.

The word 'poised' might seem like a juxtaposition. I mean the word in both contexts – being obviously ready for exceptional action should it be required but composed enough to manage the tensions in any environment with aplomb.

There are a few insights from the analysis of my approach that might be useful to consider here.

People with presence are rarely frenetic. I use careful body language with controlled gestures that display ease and purpose. You rarely see my hands or my body move in a way that seems hurried. My body language stays in a zone somewhere between my neck and my waist and only ever slightly wider than my shoulders.

I am incredibly purposeful about eye contact. Appropriate eye contact signals confidence and openness to connection (bearing in mind there are some cultural differences), but much like with engaged awareness, it's not about a clinical or transactional approach. I have seen people who teach 'presentation skills' talk about dividing the audience into quadrants and casting your eyes between those sectors. Instead, I encourage you to look at people when they are talking, when what they say moves you, when their body language indicates they agree, disagree, don't understand or have had a new thought, and when you suspect their mind has wandered, as all our minds will from time to time.

REMAINING CALM

I maintain a calm demeanour, especially when I am exercised or aggravated. This doesn't mean people are confused about whether I am disappointed or not about what's going on, but I won't allow people to move me out of a space where my mind feels supple enough to handle the challenge, and an angry mind is a stiff and rigid mind.

Self-awareness is also involved here because it enables us to better recognise and manage our emotions while empathising with others. This skill is crucial for maintaining composure and responding appropriately in challenging situations.

I don't raise my voice from anger or frustration.

Part of our presence and being seen to be present is our ability to act like a smart, connected thermostat. In addition to being aware of the temperature of a person or a group of people, you know when it's getting chilly and have tools to act so the temperature rises before anyone starts to shiver. Conversely, you can sense when the room is getting too warm and can act to counteract that before people begin to sweat.

The first element of this temperature control is yourself, and as such, I am a bigger fan of breathing exercises than I ever thought I would be.

I can sleep in any circumstance, from the back of a car to or from the airport to my own bed at night in eight seconds, using standard breathing methods like the four-box breathing technique, which you can read more about in the next chapter. We will explore practical strategies for maintaining relaxed readiness and composure and enabling the flow of one's thoughts and ideas.

GENUINE COMMUNICATION AND TRANSPARENCY

Those with authentic presence express themselves with precision and honesty.

When I was at Penn State University, I used to go into my guidance counsellor's office between classes and rifle through a dictionary, stopping at a random page and finding a new word I could learn. I was already an avid reader at that point. Reading any science fiction I could get my hands on taught me that there were banal and generic, or excitingly particular ways to describe things. I knew that choice of language made the difference between a book you never got past page 12 and a book you couldn't put down.

The first word I found and shared with Sandy was 'syllogism' (an instance of a form of reasoning in which a conclusion is drawn from two given or assumed premises).

As a result of this habit, which I still practise digitally to this day, I often know the correct word to use to describe a sentiment or idea without always being able to define it. You'd better believe I double-check the directory before I use it! But with this arsenal of honed words, even though some consider me contentious in my thoughts and declarations, I tend to be able to share my ideas, even with groups that oppose them, without unnecessarily raising hackles.

We might have a good laugh here if we consider that I'm suggesting 'I have all the best words', but I am only encouraging you if you're interested in being seen to have a presence, to obtain the words that allow you to precisely implant your intent and content in someone else's mind without misconstrual, misinterpretation or accidental defamation.

One of the ways we convey genuine transparency is through expert feedback. People broadly don't like being given unsolicited feedback, and many don't enjoy well-constructed feedback either! But when unsolicited, the recipient is likely to be more suspicious of your motives, unprepared for what you'll say, less likely to implement your suggestions, and more defensive from the outset. However, unsolicited feedback when constructed well, can be some of the kindest feedback a person gets.

Here's an example using this structure that I hear about from many HR colleagues: the colleague who smells.

I don't use this example because I think body odour intrinsically diminishes a person; I say it because we all know it's something that a surprisingly large number of people who would call someone a 'friend' or 'colleague' choose not to tell them when they smell.

There are many reasons why we think some people smell, some smell unique but acceptable, and others smell unique and unacceptable. Some are dietary, some biological (including age, which changes how we smell to others) or medical reasons, and some will be based on washing conventions or thoroughness.

I am not clear if any of these body odour outliers are necessarily related to 'professionalism', but I know managers who have chosen not to tell colleagues who smell bad to them so they can change, even as they have overlooked them for promotion or appropriate project work *because* they smell. All of these managers allowed these corrupted relationships to exist because giving feedback to fill a colleague's blind spot[5] was so hard it was worth sacrificing that colleague's career for – and that's just cruel.

Instead, a simple script can reduce the tension through pre-preparation and enable a kindness that can save someone's job, and perhaps more importantly, their dignity.

I have added this description and another example in the Principles to Practice section at the end of this chapter, but you can see its structure in this approach in Figure 2.1, and a suggestion for a conversation given this scenario that follows:

Figure 2.1   Compassionate Feedback Process

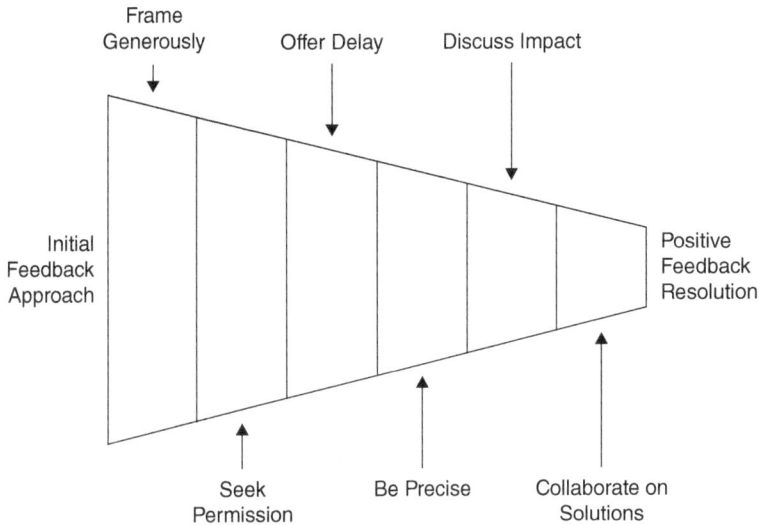

Frame: 'Hi John, I can see you're working hard, doing great work and making a good impression.'

Permission: 'I've noticed something that might be getting in the way. Can I talk to you about it?'

[option. . .] 'If now isn't a good time, I can come back to you on [actual date and time]'.

[If now . . .]

Precise and objective: 'I've noticed that you have a powerful body odour at times; I don't believe that this is a profound statement about you as a person, but . . .'

Impact: '. . .Several colleagues and clients have remarked about it in a way that negatively impacts their perception of you, and I don't want that to continue.'

Curious and open: 'I know there are many reasons, including medical conditions, that can cause this (and I am not asking you to disclose), but I am interested in stopping this from impacting people's comfort and confidence in your professionalism'.

Collaborate: 'Is there a way I can support you, as we must find a solution?'

Embrace the positives: 'You're doing excellent work. Everyone knows this; this one small challenge is the only thing getting in the way of your otherwise impeccable impression'.

Dr Shelby Hill[6] suggests that asking permission to share your thoughts is like 'a gentle knock on the door of [a person's] psyche rather than barging in' and I agree.

Please remember, it can hurt to hear even the most thoughtful critique. What you say need not be cruel, and if it is, that's a choice either to be thoughtless in preparation or malicious in intent.

EMPATHY AND CONNECTION

The ability to genuinely connect with others is a hallmark of authentic presence. This involves actively listening (something we will discuss at length in Chapter 4 – but hopefully in a way you won't have heard before!), showing interest in others' experiences, responding appropriately to other people's emotional and cognitive states, and demonstrating empathy and compassion so there is safety for substantive dialogue and, in time, disclosure.

In therapeutic settings, this connection allows for deeper understanding and more effective interventions, and although most of our interactions with others may not be therapeutic, they should be intentional – with the idea that you orient every tool at your disposal to allow others to both know that you're present and that you are a person with presence.

Being seen to have this type of presence is not about being the loudest or most extroverted person in the room. Instead, it's a subtle yet powerful quality that emerges from a combination of self-awareness, authenticity and the ability to connect meaningfully with others. It's a presence that doesn't demand attention but naturally attracts it through the individual's way of being in the world.

Principles into Practice: Making it Real
Fill Your Blind Spot; Help Another Do the Same

Seek out three or four people who care about you. They may be colleagues at work, a partner, a close friend, a mentor or a teenage relative you spend a lot of time with.

Set the scene with the following script:

'I am talking to you because I am doing some professional development work on my self-awareness, and you know me and care enough about me to support this.

(Continued)

I am looking to fill my blind spots. There will be things I do or say that have unintended impacts, or you may have seen how some people who don't know me as well have a different impression of me.

I am not looking to get names or dig dirt; I want to know what I might be doing that could be causing harm or just making the wrong impression.

If it helps, I'd happily get this feedback from you virtually, via email or text. All I ask is that you be specific about what you've seen and offer suggestions on how I can improve.'

Tips for Giving Unsolicited, but Necessary Feedback

- *Frame* your impression of them generously.
- Ask their *permission* to share your insights.
- Give them the *option* to delay until another time.
- Be *precise and objective* about the action, interaction or behaviour (and get to the point in two sentences).
- Be explicit about the positive or negative *impact*.
- Be *curious and open to a rationale* (but not an excuse) you didn't expect.
- Be *willing to collaborate* on a solution to the negative.
- Help them to see and *embrace the positives*.

Ten Things That Are Brilliant About Me

In this exercise, you will – unsurprisingly – write 10 brilliant things about you. I am not interested in sophistry, sycophancy or soliloquies here. In granular detail, just the facts of things in your wheelhouse that you do exceptionally well. Some of these must relate to your academic or vocational interest area, but this is broader self-assurance we want to explore, not just contextual confidence.

Guidance for creating quality commitments:

- Specificity and clarity: Avoid vague statements.
- Tangibility: Focus on real, observable skills or attributes.
- Objectivity: Write about yourself as you would about a mentee you cared about – fair but affirming.

Crucial rules:

- No hedging (avoid words like 'pretty', 'fairly', 'sometimes').
- No mitigation or understatement.
- No self-deprecation.

Example:

Instead of: 'I'm pretty good at public speaking'.

Write: 'I am an excellent speaker who gets effusive, positive feedback from people who hear me talk'.

Commitment: Pre-Meeting Intention Setting

For the next week, before every one-to-one or small group meeting, ask yourself: 'What do I want my people to walk away thinking and feeling?'

(Continued)

- Commit to delivering on that intention.
- After each meeting, or at least at the end of each day, reflect on how your meetings have gone relative to the previous week.
- Ask yourself: What are the differences, and what have I learned?
- Continue this for at least six weeks – real shifts in perception and behaviour require time and consistency.
- After six weeks, ask someone who has interacted with you regularly: 'Have you noticed any difference in how I run meetings or conversations?'
- Reflect again based on what they share.

CHAPTER THREE

THE 'LIBRARY OF EXPERIENCES'

IT'S NOT MAGIC. . . IT'S LIFE CATALOGUED

W hen I started practising psychology, I asked people to pay me to help them create solutions for problems they'd previously found intractable. I had what I can only now think of as an evident condescension for the details of businesses and organisations.

Some part of me had decided that psychology was so powerful that it was a substrate-agnostic solution, so I didn't bother to be curious about or 'distracted' by the nuances and distinct differences in the businesses and organisations I worked with. Whether a construction or professional services firm, a legal practice or a private or National Health Service (NHS) hospital, I treated my knowledge as enough to prevail regardless of their complex variances.

I have no idea whether I was afraid of everything I didn't know or supremely overconfident in the small amount I knew; I believed that my theoretical approach and scientific rigour would win out.

Unsurprisingly, my results were mixed. I often found myself *so* close to the right approach or answers, but I was not near enough to succeed.

I entered these rich environments so focused on being an expert that I failed to realise that every observation and every interaction was an opportunity to learn, and not just about that specific environment, but about how to adapt my approach to better support all the different environments I wanted to work in.

Architecture firms are different from legal practices; companies in the United States are different from their European counterparts; public sector organisations are different from private companies. Companies in sectors with 2% margins have systems and people that operate differently from companies in industries with 30% margins.

My prior myopia is evident to me now, and while I am not telling you that you have to know everything about every sector or company, especially if you aren't a cross-sector consultant or organisational psychologist, you can learn how to build and effectively use your range of diverse everyday experiences and knowledge, accessing and adapting them to various contexts as a means to be seen as a wise and reliable partner when new solutions to novel problems are required. I guarantee that if you don't view your working experiences as lessons to be logged and stored, you are missing insights that could both enrich your own opportunities and enhance your ability to do your job more effectively and support or inform others with more ease.

The Library of Experiences is a personal, evolving archive of moments, memories and experiences that can be recalled and the lessons and insights applied in adjacent contexts. In this context, when I talk about memory, I am not speaking of nostalgia (and I'm not knocking nostalgia – if you run a venue featuring 80s music, I will reminisce with you all night). The library is memory with purpose, interpretation and utility. It's functional recall, with the possibility of recombination, reinterpretation and novel application, and if you're anything like me, while you can play a huge role in ensuring these moments are tagged and how easily they're accessed, you'll have less control over the categorisation.

Rather than simply reliving moments, the library categorises them over time based on their potential applicability; I am sure that each of these moments gets multiple category labels for use in varied and different cases. Although I am not clear that I have proper access to the categories my own library of experiences uses, I only know that my *most* important job when I have an interaction or experience is to proactively 'tag' it as 'potentially useful; let's hold on to this'.

If you've ever played those video games where you have a back-pack for items and you pick up a random low-power 'red hat' on day one of playing, you put it on as one of the first things you found, but then it's superseded by a 'helm of gibberish' and a thousand other items, and at some point, it's forgotten in the depths of your bag. Then, in week 12, you encounter an angry, unbeatable Babelgrog that blocks your way and demands 'a special gift' to allow you to pass. You give it some of your most expensive and rare swag, and it is unswayed. Then, just as you decide it won't get any more of your stuff and begin to walk away, you remember that red hat. It meant little when you picked it up and even less now; as you give the Babelgrog your red hat, you are amazed and thrilled in equal part when, in shimmering light, it disappears, and your path ahead is clear. You had never imag-ined the red hat would be helpful for some future challenge when you picked it up, and you'd even considered dropping it every time you reorganised your swag, but nostalgia or dumb luck had spared it every time. And here, now, you proceed where else you might have stalled because of the red hat.

You may well be able to substitute the menacing Babelgrog for a particularly challenging boss and the red hat for some scrap of insight you had encountered but dismissed, disregarded or were unable to recall in time. Building your Library of Experiences can help you in the real world.

The nature of the Library of Experiences is that not every ordi-nary (or even extraordinary) experience will be useful, but it remains true that, in the real world, we are rarely prompted with the exact experience or insight that will be useful in a given moment. It emerges, whether dredged slowly and unwillingly or more proactively surfaced like the Nimüe, the Lady of the Lake, holding Excalibur out of the water.

The experiences you tag and store often teach indirectly. Like one of my favourite characters, Nanny McPhee – played in the film by national treasure, Emma Thompson – revealed: after one particularly challenging and magical exchange between Nanny McPhee and the unruly children of single father and somewhat detached parent, Mr Brown, she reported back to him at the end of an evening that, 'Lesson three is done, sir', and when he asks what that was, she replies 'To make their beds, sir'. He listens to the rare quiet in his house and tells Nanny McPhee that he thinks they've learned much more than to make their beds, to which Nanny McPhee says, 'I teach them five lessons, Mr. Brown. What they learn is up to them.'

I love this concept – the idea that what people can learn from the same experience can be very different and distinct from any named or scripted lesson; or you can learn by delayed realisation, where the context and facts of a memory or experience translate in the most unexpected ways.

I know there are teachers reading this who are screaming right now that their whole lives are spent teaching these types of indirect or delayed-realisation lessons through a myriad of subjects and moments with students, so let's take their example and use it for our benefit.

I don't bother – ever – to dwell on what some experience might be helpful for – I recognise my job in building my Library of Experiences is to log the experience and tag the memory; oftentimes, I'll repeat the experience out loud, or I'll talk about it with a friend, always without trying to understand its potential significance or utility beyond any obvious implications. But in the early days of building my Library of Experiences, most often for me, this process of tagging required writing.

Before we get into that, please note that this isn't about becoming one of those mentalists with exceptional memory and recall. I often refer to myself as having 'goldfish memory' in that I'll say something, and then seven seconds later, it's gone. (Please don't flag this section in your book for being non-scientific. I *have* seen the research that says we've wrongly impugned the memory of goldfish for years – it just works well for my analogy!)

I regularly ask my team to note novel and unique things they hear from me or their colleagues that might be noteworthy. We even ask clients if we can video my talks or speeches with them, not to broadcast them, but because my fidelity to a script varies (to say the least), and more importantly, the questions my audiences ask me are often the purest demonstrations of the Library of Experiences in action. Words spill out in contexts or combinations I may never have uttered before, which, sadly, once spoken, are again refiled and, if unprompted, inaccessible.

One of my team members once shared a quote with me that I lavished with praise as they looked increasingly nonplussed. I reiterated that I was sincere and thought it was so good that we should use it in our work with a specific client. I asked them, 'Can we use it? Who said it?' and with a withering glance, they said: 'You. You said it . . . yesterday'. I didn't remember, but luckily, one of my colleagues had tagged that experience on my behalf.

The Library of Experiences aims to be a live, accessible archive that shapes action and helps illustrate the obscure and engage where the content might otherwise be dry.

As important and relatively simple as developing your Library of Experiences is, all of its richness is mute if, when the moment comes, you, too, suffer the brain burp.

It is my contention that a lot of what's brilliant and valuable in our brains remains inaccessible not because the memory is missing or incomplete but because the mechanism or pathway to access these memories is constrained.

Most of you will have had the 'on the tip of your tongue' experience, where a word, concept or prescient point in a meeting is 'right there' and then just as quickly gone. Others will, like me, have had moments I call 'brain burps' in public (and 'brain farts' when not), when I will be in what I think is full flow only to extemporise for a second, respond to a question or be distracted by a random shiny object and immediately have absolutely no idea what I was talking about.

This happened to me when talking to Toyota North America executives in the early 2000s. I was in full flow, at a time when I still used note cards for my speeches, when I noticed a small woman enter a side door bringing in coffee and snacks for our break, and a brain burp occurred, leaving me staring at the group of expectant executives, sweat seemingly instantly expelled from every pore. I asked a sympathetic face in the front row, 'What was I just talking about?'; while he didn't know, a few of his guesses seemed to restart my brain as I flipped through cards to find a new starting point.

It's such an awkward feeling for anyone, and it's undoubtedly one of the key fears of people who need to speak in front of important stakeholders for a living.

There is, as far as I know, no certain way to ensure you never experience a brain burp or that sense that a piece of information or the perfect analogy or illustration is in the library but out of reach, but there are techniques that can stop what I call 'the clench' that is so often the cause of this inhibition.

The clench is the sensation that overtakes so many people when they *know* they know something, whether it's the answer to a question, some pertinent detail or a compelling comment to quiet a difficult stakeholder, but they can't access it in the moment.

Under those circumstances, people seem to treat their brains like a tube of toothpaste, one that, if they squeeze hard enough, the perfect amount will come out every time. But I've seen both sides: one where no amount of mashing will release even a pearl of toothpaste and one where the first squeeze produces an uncontrolled lava flow of paste.

Instead, consider that there's nothing wrong with your mind.

The knowledge and experiences you've had, whether they're tagged or not, are in there, but you are gripping so hard on the conduit between mind and voice that the flow is stifled. Anxiety, stress, external pressure and self-doubt are often exacerbated by an underdeveloped self-assurance and its associated impostor phenomenon, causing cognitive constriction, and your insights trickle rather than flood out. It's frustrating for those who might rely on your insights and expertise, and for you, who feel like you are locked out of access to your mind.

The poem by David Wagoner, called 'Lost', is how I think about access to my archive, my Library of Experiences – sometimes, when

I feel 'clenched', just reading this poem throws the doors of my library open wide.

Several techniques can provide better access to the Library and defeat 'the clench'.

If you are not predisposed to what sceptics call 'woo woo', don't worry; I am not offering anything here that doesn't have a decent evidence base behind it and that I myself use.

The first one is where the name 'Library' came from and is the one for which I have the least evidence. I don't remember when, but it was over a decade ago. I was speaking in an old building near the Noel Coward Theatre in Covent Garden, with rooms filled with books that clearly no one ever read, and I found myself reaching a place in my response to someone where a piece of information I needed was in my mind but not at my fingertips.

I only noticed as the information 'came to me' just in time that my hand was raised as if peeling back books from imaginary shelves. I have heard people talk of using 'mind palaces' as memory aids and placing information in books on imaginary shelves to remember them more readily, but that's not a technique I ever learned.

To this day, I see videos where, in response to a question, my eyes flit across a space at my eye level as if scanning for something, and my hand reaches for a book from a shelf as I speak – as if the answer is folded within the front cover. I'm not sure this is a 'good look', but it does seem to work!

Before we go on to some helpful breathing exercises, you must know that accessing the library is about understanding; I mean really embracing the reality that you *have* lived a rich enough life to have *something* in there that will work at this moment and remaining certain of that regardless of how quickly you can come to it in the early days. Without this certainty, the breathing technique seems slower to unclench the mind.

As I learned to use these breathing techniques, I paused any activity I participated in to develop the excellent insight I knew was in my head, and all too often, I had to move on from it when it didn't come to me in time. In those days, I would regularly be wrenched from bed at two in the morning, as the insight screamed in my ear – better late than never, I suppose.

Now, I have become a proponent of some simple breathing techniques. They really work for me for this unclenching purpose and for a broad range of other advantages. These techniques help with *stress reduction*,[1] *focus*[2] and *emotional regulation*,[3] and many high-performers, from business and clinical environments to *elite athletes in sports*,[4] use these techniques in the midst of their most crucial moments.

After my first sweaty forays into public forgetfulness, I recognised that my amygdala went into overdrive – something that will *not* lead to positive results. So, to counter that, I knew I needed some proven methods for dealing with amygdala hijack. I call it four-box breathing (but it's also called 'box breathing' or 'square breathing' and sometimes 'tactical breathing' in military environments).

I love doing this. Over the years, I learned to use it to calm and unclench my mind, and now, as readily as it can help me access my Library of Experiences, it helps me clear my mind and prepare for rest or sleep. You will find a million other modifications of this, but this is the version I use.

The technique involves four equal phases of breathing, each lasting the same amount of time (typically 4 seconds, but this can vary based on individual preference). Here's how it is performed:

1. Inhale: Breathe deeply through your nose for four seconds.
2. Hold: Hold your breath for four seconds.
3. Exhale: Slowly exhale through your mouth for four seconds.
4. Hold: Pause and hold your breath again for four seconds before repeating the cycle.

When I first began, I almost always had to stop what I was doing to practice this. I'd close my eyes and imagine the box with a light moving along each side as I breathed in, held my breath, breathed out and held my breath. Nowadays, I close my eyes when I have the space and time, but more typically, I engage in breathing exercises, eyes open and when engaged in my everyday work. I have done it while teaching, speaking, consulting and typing this book at my desk. I've even done interviews while four-box breathing. There's a Piers Morgan interview from the 2000s that I did while four-box breathing my way through every part where I wasn't talking!

Next, we have 'straw breathing'. Some advocate using an actual straw, but I haven't used this technique.

- Take a deep full breath in through the nose.
- Purse your lips as if there was a straw in your mouth.
- Blow out in a measured way as if you were attempting to blow gentle bubbles in a liquid with the straw.
- Repeat for two minutes

It's not one of my favourites, but it's a good option for when you think the four-box method might be a bit obvious!

Next is 'candle breathing'. It is similar to the straw-blowing method, but involves:

- Breathe out all of the air from your lungs.
- Breathe in deeply, through your nostrils only.
- Purse your lips as if you were going to blow out a candle while breathing out all of the air from your lungs (it should make a quiet shhh-ing sound).
- Hold for one second, then repeat for two minutes.

Notably, a lot of the time you want access to your Library of Experiences, you won't be on the spot; in need of an immediate response, it will simply be a small frustration as you are getting on with your work. In these moments, it's worth taking advantage of our capacity for background processing. There is a lot of data helping us see how good sleep can help us relax and reorganise our thoughts, but it can also help ease the library's opening.

Whether watering the plants in your home or home office or getting up to make a cup of tea, you can use these habitual moments of focus on the minutiae. The British army used this technique of making tea, and one example involves soldiers during World War II in the provocatively titled book *Who Ordered This Truckload of Dung? Inspiring Stories for Welcoming Life's Difficulties*[5] by Ajahn Brahm, where a British patrol in Burma under impending attack, was ordered to sit down and make tea instead of engaging in a desperate fight, giving them time to calm their minds, think clearly, and ultimately devise a plan to escape safely.

I now understand that if I give myself seven seconds, breathe using one of these techniques and 'unclench', then nine times out of ten, the word, information or example will cruise out, announcing itself to my brain as it comes.

This whole chapter – indeed, this entire book – is an example of the Library of Experiences in action.

Each of the following memories surfaced without my provocation, seemingly in response to the urgency of the moment – the ideas I was attempting to illustrate and make more real for you.

That Christmas, nearly twenty years ago, I watched Nanny McPhee while wrapping presents, and that memorable scene struck me somewhere between sellotape and ribbons. 1985, when I watched the film *Excalibur* cross-legged in my living room, I tagged the scene where Perceval angrily throws Excalibur back into the lake, and the Lady of the Lake catches it before disappearing into the water. I also tagged the David Wagoner poem 'Lost' that I heard about a decade ago in a car on the way to Oxford, read by a celebrity fan. There's the speech for Toyota and every other example you've read or will read in this book, a product of the Library of Experiences in service of illustrating points with clarity and a bit of colour.

This is not magic; this is a skill you can acquire and utilise as, if not more, effectively than me.

Principles into Practice: Making it Real
The Seven Seconds Rule

The goal is to be able to unclench in seven seconds or better.

When faced with a 'brain burp' or tip-of-the-tongue moment – those moments where you know you know something but are failing to recall it:

- Proactively use one of the breathing techniques to clear the path for your thoughts.
- Learn to understand how long each rotation of the breathing exercise (each four-box breathing circuit, for example) takes so you can understand how long it takes for the library doors to open.
- You can recite a small internal mantra, such as 'It's in here, relax', which helps my brain wait more patiently at the library door.
- *Do not* punish yourself if, as you learn this technique, you are woken hours later remembering something you'd previously been unable to recall.
- *Always* reward yourself for success. If you begin the unclenching ritual and before you've even begun, it's come to you, that's a success. If it takes 10 minutes of breathing, that's success.

Remember to practise the breathing exercises on their own, in moments of stress or brief moments of quiet, whether drinking tea in the morning, for a few minutes of your commute, while running or at the gym, or a moment between meetings. You'll habituate the breathing routine so that your mind doesn't need to focus on it and the unclenching simultaneously.

Activities to Tag and Build Your Library of Experience

The daily debrief (five minutes)

- At the end of each day, write down one experience, interaction or response that surprised, frustrated or intrigued you. You may have experienced, been part of, or simply observed it.
- Add a 'Possible Use' category for the experience if you can think of one readily, but don't spend too much time on that: e.g., *This might help me when . . .*
- Take a look at the table below for options, but bear in mind that the detail in the 'what happened' column, along with a name for the experience, are the most important elements to ensure the experience is tagged.

The tag and park system

- Use a notes app, spreadsheet or even voice memos.
- When something feels significant, note it and give a categorisation if that comes easily (e.g., 'power shift', 'trust issues', 'team dynamics') without needing full clarity.
- Commit to revisiting your list monthly.
- Choose a recent experience from the list and mentally 'replay' it.

(Continued)

- If new categorisations occur, note them, or if an application relevant to your current situation comes to mind, note that for deployment.

I just had a long bullet list, but I always gave my anecdotes, experiences and memories names to enhance the memory tagging process. But if you prefer something more structured, consider modifying the following table as a starting point.

Date	What Happened? (Detail and give it a name)	Important Emotional Elements	Categories	Recurring? Note when happens again	How Could This Be Useful?
04/04/2025	'BOSS SHUT DOWN': A junior team member contradicted me in a meeting but was probably right. I didn't respond as if they were right and cut the conversation, telling them we'd 'take it offline'. They were visibly disappointed.	Defensive, then curious	Ego, team trust, challenge	12/05/2025 – saw this in client team too	Could help me stay open when direct reports challenge my perspective in high stakes conversations

CHAPTER FOUR

THE ART OF PERCEPTIVE LISTENING

IT'S NOT MAGIC. . . IT'S CONNECTION

THE ILLUSION OF LISTENING

Experience tells me that the default for most contexts where people gather intentionally is that they don't listen to each other. This isn't because not enough people have been trained in active listening or too many people are 'busy', but rather because we increasingly exist in a world where what we each think, no matter how unexamined, is more unique, meaningful and worthy of broadcast than what other people think. Consequently, what other people think is more unimportant to us than ever, and choosing to listen to others becomes a function of harm avoidance or personal affirmation.

Harm avoidance encapsulates those moments when we must listen to people (those with power over us), lest our obvious lack of engagement cost us in some way we consider important – that can be in the domains of everything from career progression to social credibility ('cool points').

We listen to people for personal affirmation by finding (or succumbing to an algorithm that does it for us) people whose narratives and authority (often only embraced because they agree with you) reinforce our opinions or ideas to give us a greater sense of conviction and righteousness. Interestingly, this type of affirmation spreads beyond any single idea being validated at that moment, but by extension, all the ideas, no matter how unrelated, we may have sequestered in our heads.

These changes are systemic and may seem an odd place to start a chapter on listening, but these shifts significantly influence the broad conventions and norms of speaking to each other and, thereby, our approach to listening to one another.

The current cultural and political zeitgeist suggests that, at least nominally, a 'free speech absolutist' approach should be the norm. The idea is that in our inner world (and any other world that 'matters'), every voice that rises to prominence does so out of objective, bias-free merit.

It also means that people should say everything they think. In this new world, it's up to the recipients of these messages to demonstrate their worthiness and resilience and 'handle' whatever messages come their way.

Many now consider any negative or damaging impact of what they say to others to be a function of weakness on the part of the recipient rather than thoughtlessness or ruthlessness on their own part. You may think this is about orange autocrats, space-obsessed 'tech bro's' or social media 'fact-checking' fails, but it's in our homes and offices too – when one partner in a relationship insists it's always 'their way or the highway'; or where managers hurl their disapproval at fresh graduates as if they were the knife throwers' assistant, bound not to flinch should they be nicked and always blamed for spoiling the show when the audience can see their blood.

We're in an era of 'sonic libertarianism' now. *Sonic libertarianism is a concept I use to explain* the sociocultural phenomenon where individuals operate within, yet deliberately ignore, the shared communicative environment. That is, where there's an aggressive disregard for how messages reverberate and resonate within social spaces and a speaker's right to express is treated as absolute – a right and a virtue – and where any hostile or antagonistic reception is considered an inherent weakness in any individual listener and a universal pathology in any group that objects.

This mindset reflects a radical individualism in modern discourse where the speed and force of expression override considerations of reception or harm, treating communication as a unidirectional force rather than a reciprocal exchange – an era where what others think is more unimportant to us than ever before, and any damaging impacts of what we say to others is deemed a personal failing of the recipient rather than a matter of communicative responsibility.

This is a devastating approach to communicating with colleagues at work, students at school or university or your relationships with family or partners at home and it's had a disastrous effect on how we listen to each other, how effectively we hear each other and how much of what we hear, we retain.

We need a new approach to the communication dialectic.[1] I recommend *sonic stewardship* as a counteracting approach to sonic libertarianism that recognises and actively respects the accountabilities of a shared communicative environment. Where individuals demonstrate a conscious awareness of how their messages reverberate and resonate within social spaces and where a speaker's right to express is balanced with their responsibility to the broader communicative ecosystem. This mindset reflects a collaborative approach to modern discourse where the quality and impact of expression are given equal weight to the act of expression itself, treating communication as a reciprocal exchange that requires mutual investment and care. It represents an era where the thoughtful consideration of others' perspectives enriches our own understanding and where the impact of our communication is viewed as a shared responsibility requiring both speakers' mindful expression and listeners' engaged reception.

It's interesting to me that when I first moved to America, I heard a lot in civics classes about free speech and its limits – especially the 'you can't yell "fire!" in a crowded theatre' example.

Notwithstanding that it appears that lots of prominent people have been yelling (never mind fanning) 'fire' in public spaces. The limitation this exception implies is an example of sonic stewardship.

THE SELFISH THOUGHT

'You're not listening to me; you're waiting for me to finish so you can continue to speak.'

No week goes by in any working month where I don't say this to someone, usually, multiple times as they look at me with micro-utterances and objections, blurting out fragments of denial left and right. In group coaching or teaming sessions, the tension can be palpable as an entire room realises that this is their status quo:

They don't listen to each other. They take turns speaking.

You've done this, I've done this, we've all been guilty. But instead of miring ourselves in that guilt, let's galvanise and do something about it. Guilt is an inherently selfish emotion. It tends to focus on how 'bad' *we* feel about something 'bad' that *we've* done. Instead, we're going to stop doing it by understanding why we do it and some techniques and tools to catch ourselves.

There are factors that make it more likely that we won't listen to others.

Power Dynamics

There are differentials of power in every environment. These can be based on a combination of variously important criteria that include specific technical or contextual experience, tenure (literally, just having been around for a long time) and affinity, the sense that either the similarity and familiarity of the person speaking or the content being discussed warrant different attention.

Where listeners have a great experience, they may very quickly dismiss submissions from others they deem to have less. This can happen when they see the meeting invite and agenda and well before they step into a real or virtual room.

People with less experience can also find truly listening to submissions from experts challenging. Instead of listening, they may try to create pertinent questions or sensible and praiseworthy comments that demonstrate they understood what was shared if asked by someone of consequence or the speaker themselves.

I remember being invited to one of the *BBC Reith Lectures*[2] a decade or more ago. These are truly prestigious, nationally broadcast, live seminars featuring the eminent scientists, philosophers and thinkers of our age. I sat in the front row (it was a legroom issue rather than a reflection of the esteem I am held by the BBC), and I scribbled thoughts and ideas because what I heard was new and unfamiliar. As the Q&A section began, a microphone was manoeuvred into my face, and the newsreader who was playing host said, 'I saw you writing furiously; you must have a question.'

I had a thousand questions and no idea what I wanted to ask at that moment; I had been listening and writing to help process, but not to ask. So I asked something, and the speaker refuted the premise of my question before answering a different, and more interesting tangential question of their own.

There was no malice intended here, but it is the kind of experience in a workplace, for example, that might remind you to prepare to avoid embarrassment rather than really listen to the material being shared. I haven't been invited back to a Reith lecture since then, but I'm choosing not to believe I shamed myself so grievously that I am *persona non grata*!

Ego is another problem for listening.

Sometimes, there are so many 'smartest people (usually men) in the room' that I am at a loss to understand why the world of work, academia and politics have so many problems. In truth, we know that when clever people get together to prove their cleverness, intellectual sword-fighting ensues and everyone gets drenched, but not in anything good.

Ego can contribute to zero-sum game thinking, where engagement with other people is about winning, not solutions. Ego can make the goal of a conversation the cleverest and most devastating mic-drop or ad hominem attack rather than anything substantive or constructive.

Ego and drinking the Kool-Aid of your own intellectual supremacy also contribute to 'anticipation overconfidence' – the idea that you know the kind of thing a person will contribute and you know you won't value it, so you are now free to consider your own thoughts and next statements, rather than listening to what is being offered.

Ego is also responsible for the need to appear confident, which in many Western cultures is defined by how much of the time you are heard speaking in any meeting.[3] A study in 2021 suggested that proportionate speaking time and physical expressiveness significantly affected performance evaluations more than task competence. People have picked up this message, meaning listening carefully and reflecting to create a cogent response may get you overlooked in the face of a colleague who has decided to forgo listening to generate an animated and immediate, if only tangentially related, diatribe.

There are boring logistical reasons, too, for why we don't listen.

Time pressure and the burdens of back-to-back utilisation cultures impact preparedness. They can mean that we come into meetings aware that we must quickly read essential content while we listen to a speaker.

Even those fun 'working lunches' set us up to fail, and they are often done with kindness in mind. To be 'efficient', we offer food and drink as the meeting starts, so listening and attention are split between the content of focus and the questions about which sandwiches are vegan and which coffee is decaf.

We invite people into meeting rooms who have little experience and no active role in the agenda. We do this in the name of 'learning', but we continue to speak at a pace and complexity that fogs their brains and leaves them questioning what just happened to them.

While explicitly stating well-being and 'mindfulness' principles, cultural norms in many organisations implicitly demand ongoing multitasking and a relentless cognitive load that means colleagues forego listening for scripting an upcoming conversation with a client or manager, catching up on another project deadline or just maintaining their inbox zero count.

If you're serious about listening, the sonic orientation and logistical adjustments are all straightforward fixes.

Tool: Meeting Framing (as a Meeting Leader)

State What's Expected

In every meeting, participants should know what's on the agenda and how they are expected to interact with the items. We listen in a different way if we are being informed without the expectation of quizzing or on-the-spot brilliance.

Are they to contribute to the discussion, offer solutions, listen to be informed or something else?

Is contribution welcome regardless of whether or not it agrees with the status quo?

Tell People What You Value

For example:

'I want us all to concentrate on active and undistracted listening'.

'I value considered responses over the fastest reply'.

'I am happy if any or all of you need time to reflect in the meeting before responding'.

'I would rather have a response or idea from you that targets part of our shared problem than no response at all'.

Set Ground Rules

Consider codifying meetings with basic courtesies such as: 'We do not talk over each other'.

You can encourage using the '2-second beat' – literally granting two seconds of silence after a statement from a colleague before responding to a colleague or using consent statements, such as: 'I've got some thoughts/questions if you've finished yours?'

Encourage tactics that allow people to retain spontaneous ideas without interrupting. I have an e-ink tablet next to my computer that I use to jot down ideas that occur so I can free myself up to continue to listen with the briefest interruption and retain a thought that – for me, at least – usually evaporates if un-noted.

Other colleagues of mine use the 'put a finger down' technique, where they put a finger on a table – this is not some over-dramatic, sweeping flourish that interrupts the flow of a speaker; it simply helps them to hold a thought for a short time in that purposeful action, so they can relay their insight when the speaker is finished without that thought dominating their mind. The benefit of this practice is that, over time, colleagues start to notice the subtle movement of their index finger on a table or, to a lesser extent, their note-taking. And it signals the need for conciseness or a pause to allow a new insight to emerge.

If we're serious about enabling effective listening, we should acknowledge that not everyone is neurotypical. Cognitive styles and accessibility barriers can also hinder listening.

I coached a FTSE executive whose brilliance was unquestionable but whose cognitive idiosyncrasies meant that the company convention of presenting volumes – literally thousands of pages – of dense slide content in board meetings meant they couldn't effectively listen in the meetings due to cognitive overwhelm. A simple change by the Chair, demanding concise and prioritised bullet points in meetings and summarised, more to-the-point pre-board packs, had this individual listening more effectively and able to contribute maximally.

As with most examples of change driven by a desire to accommodate differences, these modifications reduced the noise and clutter of meetings, focused attention and allowed the entire board to listen, challenge, collaborate and communicate more effectively.

These are just a few techniques and ideas to consider, and I'll encourage you to make one personal and one logistical or structural change to improve your listening and the ability of others to listen around you in the commitment section. As always, these commitments are quarterly – make them, integrate them, habituate them for you and others, and then find a new commitment to augment your goals further.

Before that, we should consider some personal factors in listening without repeating everything you might have read in more detail in a thousand other books or articles covering active listening.

On a personal level, effective listening requires a desire to be wrong – not just to be educated or curious but to embrace in a moment, perhaps one-to-one, but very often with a group, that you are wrong.

I went to a meeting at what was then UCLAN (the University of Central Lancashire) in Preston, the North of England, to talk with some lecturers about a course I devised based on Daniel Goleman's original 'emotional intelligence' work. At the time, I was all in on

Goleman's original 1990s model (but I wasn't meeting these educators in 1990!) I'd proposed a syllabus for executives, and very early on, I realised I was not the only expert in the room. Actually, I realised I was not an expert in the room.

I received a thoughtfully delivered torrent of new information, perspectives and insights that really hurt because it challenged everything I had grown comfortable with and based my work on. In a somewhat juvenile revelation – everything that was my 'truth' about emotional intelligence was wrong.

You could say 'not fit for purpose', 'not evolved', 'not nuanced enough', or any other kindly contortion, but I think I listened and learned in that interaction in part because those colleagues were kind and thoughtful in their approach. However, I also knew quickly that I was wrong. I was wrong, but if I listened with real intent, every sentence brought me closer to being less wrong in the near future.

Listening requires vulnerability and boldness combined – a willingness to change one's mind and publicly cede power when something someone mentions adds perspective or supersedes your understanding.

Listen to the Whole Person

One of the myths of listening is the Mehrabian Myth. In the mid-1960s Albert Mehrabian devised a model that people took to explain all communication and what parts of communication were really important – you will have heard some version of it:

'x% of communication is body language' or
'Only x% of communication is transmitted in the words'.

Less well understood as the myth took hold was that these 'rules' described emotional and persuasive speech more than everyday interactions.

For our purposes here, it's important only to recognise that what we are attending to as good listeners needs to embrace the words chosen, the tone and inflexion spoken, and the nonverbal body language conveyed.

It feels like a dizzying onslaught of things to notice, as if you need to be one of the experts from *Criminal Minds* or the deception experts from the show *Lie to Me* to be able to gather and condense all this input. I was originally tempted – in part, because I love those programmes – to dazzle you with insights I've learned from listening to behavioural analysis experts, but you don't need to know forensic interviewing techniques to be a great listener.

But there are a few keys I have learned to embrace from their discipline. Look for combined clusters of words, tone and behavioural cues that might indicate a more nuanced understanding of a message. Force yourself to attend to each word, how it's said and any body language accompanying it. Don't be distracted by that one thing you saw Patrick Jane say was a clear 'tell' for deceit on a random episode of *The Mentalist*. We are, by nature, creatures who love a shortcut, and if we allow ourselves to believe that we can ignore 95% of interaction so long as we spot that one telling gesture, then true listening will continue to go the way of the dodo.

While you can't manufacture the perception of listening, you can make listening easier for yourself. There is some evidence that less frequent and longer eye fixations are more associated with a focus on internal thoughts. If you're anything like me, if I stare at someone or something for too long, I inevitably end up inside my head rather than focusing on the person or item in front of me. So instead, I aim for shorter eye fixations, seeing the whole person but allowing what they show me from moment to moment, with gestures, tone, language and their own eye contact to direct my eyes.

Spot the Incongruences in Messaging

This was a key element of Michelle's research. She told me that I 'listen for and spot cognitive dissonance and emotional incongruity in others' comments, and between their body language and words'.

I think people believe I do this by forensically examining every individual syllable, eye flutter or pursed lip, but I'm just not capable of that amount of processing power – at least not at pace.

I have become good at hearing whole people when I talk to them – I rarely focus on one eye, one fidgeting foot or a random spot in the middle of their forehead. Whether I am in person or virtual, I allow my eyes to see a whole person and 'fixate' (read: look at a part of the person in front of me carefully, but not for too long, before moving on). For the most part, I focus on the face, but I know it's important to see what else is going on in a virtual cube or the whole person across from me if I really want to be able to hear what's being said.

In hearing the whole person, I am really looking at 'message clusters'. Message clusters are the tapestry of signals we receive from others during communication – a combination of words chosen, how they're delivered, and the physical signals that accompany them. Unlike traditional models of communication that treat these elements separately, message clusters recognise that meaning emerges from the interplay between verbal content (specific word choices and patterns), paralinguistic features (tone, pace, volume), and non-verbal signals (posture, gestures, facial expressions).

The key to understanding message clusters and noticing incongruences isn't just observing these elements but establishing a 'personal baseline'. These are the typical communication patterns unique to each individual in a specific context. This baseline allows us to spot meaningful deviations that might signal important shifts in emotion, conviction or intent.

The power of message clusters lies in detecting subtle incongruencies, such as when one element shifts while others remain consistent with the baseline. For instance, when a senior executive maintains their usual measured tone and relaxed posture while discussing quarterly results, but their typically fluid hand gestures become more constrained, or when a team member's characteristic word choice and animation remain unchanged, but their voice takes on a barely perceptible tightness during specific topics. These small deviations within an otherwise consistent cluster often signal important underlying messages that might be missed by focusing on more obvious changes. This approach moves beyond the oversimplified percentages often quoted about communication (like the misapplied Mehrabian model) and instead focuses on what actually matters: the subtle changes in an individual's usual communication pattern that signal something worthy of our attention.

In almost every consequential conversation I have, I want to understand a baseline for each individual. I am not doing this to 'profile' them but to allow a more tailored approach to listening to them and – hopefully – to prevent me from missing something important as they speak to me.

Again, I don't expect everyone from every background to have the same message cluster combination. Noticing gaps and incongruences, while informative, especially over the course of a longer relationship, is not mind-reading. If you use this technique, you must be disciplined and resist the temptation to think every deviation from the norm is important.

Sometimes, a banana is just a banana.

Clarify the Incongruences

When we listen, we aren't looking for incongruences as a 'gotcha' but rather to better understand the nuance of the message. That's why we should – at the right time – and without accusation, blame or judgment, use clarifying questions to address the incongruences you see and the lack of transparency that usually inspires.

These are not unique questions, but you can see some examples here in different scenarios. I have included some 'managing up' scenarios as I know that many of you will interact with people with power over your career.

Most often in the workplace, the elements of the message cluster that are mismatched are a tone and physicality that don't match the scripted words they're saying. Here's how we might respond in some of those situations:

- Mirroring their energy: 'I hear what you're saying about being confident with the timeline, and I want to ensure I'm fully supporting this. Could we talk through what success looks like at each stage?'

- Acknowledging the weight: 'This is clearly a significant change. Could you help me understand which elements you think deserve our closest attention?'
- Creating space: 'I sense there might be more to consider here. Would it be helpful to take a moment to explore the broader implications?'

These work because they respond to the full message cluster rather than just the verbal content while still allowing the more senior person to choose their level of disclosure. They can, of course, ignore the lifeline you've given them, but regardless of their action, they will know you *really* heard them.

Get Feedback on Your Listening

This can feel intimidating. As I mentioned in previous chapters, our assessment of ourselves often falls prey to overly generous or overly critical thinking. However, knowing how you are perceived is important. I looked at some of the key elements that indicate effective listening. While this inventory is far from comprehensive, it is a tool key stakeholders can use to assess how you're perceived as a listener quickly.

A little preamble will be necessary when you make this ask of a colleague, manager, friend or partner:

'I am not looking for your generosity or for you to use your knowledge of how much I care or how busy you think I am as excuses. I want to become an engaged, active listener, and I need your help and insights to understand where I am and how I might improve.

Please be as objective as possible and score me based on my normal listening baseline, not just those great days when I am focused or those bad days when I am distracted. Score me on my average over a month.

When it's done, I'll take some time to understand, and I'd love to ask you about specific ways I can improve our communication."

The tool is in the Principles into Practice section, along with a grid that highlights the kind of missteps you might be making to give you a head start on that introspection. Remember that it is more of a discussion starter than a final test. If you score poorly in a dimension, it's a good idea to take time to reflect on what you did that you think caused that score and then do some gentle questioning that focuses on practical behaviours you can change.

If you speak to a few people in each context over time, you can see how you are viewed in these different contexts.

Consider if it's not the same everywhere, why isn't it?

For all of you who've been 360-degree surveyed to death, I'd recommend you treat these as micro-insights into the specific contexts where you've tapped people to share their thoughts – if trends appear in some contexts, interrogate them and see if those stakeholders can shed light on what you do or not that has created the impression you get in feedback.

Hearing from multiple people with different perspectives can be useful, but don't make the mistake many make, which is to imagine that three (or more) subjective opinions will somehow create one objective fact.

EMPOWERING THE SPEAKER: LISTENING AS LEADERSHIP

Before we end this chapter on listening, I want to emphasise that perceptive listening is an act of empowerment for the person talking.

As a teenager, I remember sitting in my headmaster's study with my Mum at my side; I had decided not to play one of the two 'elite' sports that my school offered – rugby and (if you can believe it) lacrosse. Instead, I would play basketball – something my head-teacher called 'a poor person's sport'. As a 6 foot 9 inch 'number 8' on the school's first team, this choice was not sitting well with him.

I had rehearsed my words and role-played them with my mother, but now she sat next and slightly angled towards me rather than my headteacher. She smiled as I began, and she nodded as I made my points, and it felt like her focus never left me, except when the head sat forward early in my exposition and looked like he was going to interrupt me, and at that moment, her eyes darted to him for an immeasurably tiny fraction of a second before he leant back palms raised in surrender, and allowed me to finish.

I never played rugby again after that day. Just being there to really listen to someone is an act of solidarity. It supports enhanced psychological safety and encourages boldness, and – as in the example I just described – it can be the difference between someone finishing their thought or not.

In the next chapter, we will address the role of personal vulnerability in empowering others, but the Venn diagram nature of leadership characteristics means elements overlap. Listening, too, can be a core element of empowerment for the people around us, and if you can make people feel safer to stretch themselves, bolder in their declarations, and more valued as people, it's not surprising this simple – and definitely not magic – aspect can be such a difference-maker.

Principles into Practice: Making it Real
Activity: What Is the Predominant 'Sonic Orientation' of Your Key Environments?

Definitions:

- *Sonic Libertarianism:* The practice of communicating with wilful disregard for how one's messages affect shared spaces, treating the right to express as absolute whilst dismissing any antagonistic reception as the listeners' weakness. This approach views communication as one-directional, prioritising speed and force of expression over consideration of impact or harm. The listener is cast as either irrelevant or solely responsible for managing their own reaction, expected to absorb or deflect without protest. Denied meaningful agency, their discomfort is re-framed as fragility rather than as feedback, and they often withdraw, self-censor, or develop defensive interpretive habits to preserve their psychological safety.
- *Sonic Stewardship:* The practice of communicating with conscious awareness of how one's messages affect shared

---

spaces, balancing expression rights with responsibilities to the communicative ecosystem. This approach treats communication as reciprocal, giving equal weight to quality and impact of expression, and viewing communicative responsibility as shared between speakers and listeners. Listeners in this state are regarded as co-stewards of the communicative space, with their reactions seen as valid and instructive to the speaker. They are thoughtful and proactive in engaging with curiosity and accountability, recognising their role in co-creating clarity, care, and understanding.

Think about your home and social contexts, as well as your work or academic context.

- Which sonic orientation do you experience most of the time? Describe it.
  - Who do you think is responsible? Is it any one person more than others or is it just 'the norm?'
  - Is it satisfactory? Would you be happier or more effective if it were different?
  - How might it be better?
  - What can you control or influence to shift the orientation?
- Is the sonic orientation different at home versus work or in different offices?
- Do you have the same orientation with your parents as with your teenagers?
- Does your work team operate differently from the organisation as a whole? Could it?

(Continued)

People can read all the articles on active listening they want. If they have fallen into the mindset and approach of sonic libertarianism, they won't be able to listen.

Message Cluster Baseline Assessment

Start with two to three key stakeholders in different contexts (e.g., personal and professional). For each person, reflect on:

Typical communication patterns:

- What is their natural speaking pace and volume in casual (non-presentation) conversation?
- How do they typically use silence or pauses?
- What are their characteristic gestures or movements when relaxed?
- Where do they tend to position themselves in relation to others?

Contextual variations:

- How do their patterns shift between formal and informal settings?
- What changes do you notice when they're under time pressure?
- How do their patterns differ when speaking to individuals versus groups?

Language choice and patterns:

- What is their characteristic vocabulary in relaxed settings?
- Do they consistently use particular phrases or expressions?

- How does their language formality shift across different contexts?
- What is their typical level of precision in word choice?

Physical response patterns:

- What are their characteristic breathing patterns when at ease?
- How does their complexion typically respond to different situations?
- What are their usual patterns of physical tension or release?
- How do they physically respond to agreement or disagreement?

Personal tells:

- What subtle changes have you noticed precede important news or difficult conversations?
- Are there specific topics that consistently trigger small shifts in their usual pattern?
- What behavioural changes signal they're truly engaged versus going through the motions?

Reflection questions:

- How confident are you in your knowledge of their baselines?
- Which aspects of their communication do you feel least certain about?
- What gaps in your observation become apparent through this exercise? (How often have you said, 'I don't know?')

(Continued)

Listening Effectiveness Assessment

1 = Completely Disagree
2 = Disagree
3 = Agree
4 = Completely Agree

Q1. Do I give you my full attention when we're speaking? (Do I show effective eye contact, engage actively in the content with you, and avoid being easily distracted?)

Q2. Do I make you feel understood during our conversations? (Do I paraphrase your statements, validate your points, and ask clarifying questions?)

Q3. Do I avoid interrupting or rushing you to respond? (Do I demonstrate patience when you are talking, allowing space for your full thoughts and allowing for moments of silence?)

Q4. Do I follow up or act on what you share with me? (Do I reference past discussions in a way that makes it clear I heard and remembered what you've said in the past? Do I complete actions that we agree from conversations without prompting?)

Q5. Please consider how I might improve or any particular behaviours that reduce the sense I am listening.

(Please share your answers with me within a week and if you have anything else to add, please let me know in whatever way you find most comfortable – in person or virtually, via WhatsApp, Messages, Zoom or Teams, etc.)

Listening Effectiveness Scoring

The table below helps assess listening effectiveness based on feedback from others using a simple scoring system. Use the score ranges to identify which type of listener you are and receive tailored feedback for improvement.

Score range	Listener type	Description	Feedback
15–16	Engaged active listener	– Demonstrates full attention and active engagement. – Shows understanding through paraphrasing and clarifying questions. – Avoids interruptions and allows for complete thoughts. – Follows up and acts on information shared.	'Your listening skills are exemplary. You create a space where people feel valued, understood, and empowered to share openly. Keep reinforcing these habits and model them for others'.
12–14	Attentive passive listener	– Pays attention and shows engagement. – May understand but doesn't actively demonstrate it. – Rarely interrupts but doesn't actively encourage elaboration. – May remember information but doesn't consistently follow up.	'You're attentive and engaged but could enhance your impact by actively showing understanding (e.g., paraphrasing) and following through on shared information'.

(Continued)

Score range	Listener type	Description	Feedback
8–11	Distracted listener	– Attention wavers and engagement is inconsistent. – May miss key points or misunderstand due to lack of clarification. – Occasionally interrupts or rushes responses. – Often forgets details and rarely follows up.	'You may be present in conversations, but distractions or lack of active listening behaviours can lead to misunderstandings or missed opportunities. Focus on being fully present and showing your understanding more explicitly.'
4–7	Disengaged listener	– Shows minimal attention or engagement. – Frequently misunderstands or ignores speaker's points. – Often interrupts or dominates the conversation. – Rarely retains information or acts on what's shared.	'Your listening behaviours may make others feel undervalued or unheard. Consider making an intentional effort to reduce distractions, avoid interruptions, and act on what is shared with you.'

Based on what you've learned, what actions are you going to take? As a leader of meetings where you want people to listen, what can you do logistically and functionally in and around the meeting context to enable that?

What personal commitments will you make as a meeting participant to ensure you are seen as a perceptive listener?

PART II

ELEVATING EVERYDAY LEADERSHIP

CHAPTER FIVE

EMPOWERMENT THROUGH VULNERABILITY

IT'S NOT MAGIC. . . IT'S CREDIBILITY

Vulnerability in leadership is uncomfortable, or perhaps more accurately, disquieting, for leaders who are so used to the perception of omniscience that comes with their tenure or title. However, vulnerability is not a soft concession; it is a strategic act that builds credibility, strengthens relationships, and fosters high performance as Brené Brown alludes to in her book, *Daring Greatly*.[1]

However, in many organisations, even asking questions and clarifying understanding can be seen as a form of unwelcome vulnerability, with any colleague bold enough to ask wearing a virtual 'dunce hat' for the rest of the year.

In most organisations, filling in gaps in knowledge or clarifying your understanding is seen as indicating vulnerability, and while I don't think asking questions should feel vulnerable, I am *not* one of those people who believes there are no stupid questions or, perhaps more accurately, I think there are questions that make the person asking them appear stupid.

In my last book, *The Promises of Giants*, I spoke about the 'Three Before Me' protocol that my team employs, not because any of us are aloof or too important to answer questions, but because if your question can be answered in a simple Internet search, it's not a good use of another human's time.

It's a different case where a new colleague is unsupported and doesn't even know the right questions to ask, which is why comprehensive induction and in-house mentors should exist!

However, the difference between questions that make the asker appear uninformed and those that make them sound professional is framing.

There are 'enhancing' versus 'stultifying' ways to be vulnerable where asking questions is concerned.

Here are some examples:

- When you talk about 'trying' to do something, please remember that Yoda was right when he said, 'Do or do not; there is no try'.
- 'Try' often implies that we have failed to understand or have missed information, which reduces our confidence in accomplishing something. Instead of centring your statement on doubt, focus on asking for the information you need to fill the knowledge gap.
- 'I am missing *X* information/process/insight I need to complete this' or 'I will need *Y* to complete this. Can someone tell me where I can find this?'
- Even when the doubt is a practical one where you don't want to be seen as lazy or inefficient by your boss, but you know you're being asked to deliver an additional task that can't all get done, instead of saying, 'There's no way I can finish all these things on deadline!' (regardless of how true that is!), instead, say something more like, 'I have an existing priority request [from *X* person] with a deadline of *DD*; do I have permission to re-prioritise this new task, understanding that means I will complete the existing request *X* days/hours later'.

In this last example, you are again reframing the vulnerability from some supposed missing quality in you (tenacity, diligence, etc.) to a genuine uncertainty about prioritisation.

I like Molly Graham's work, which, among other things, discusses the virtues of being a 'professional idiot'. I think this is valuable in theory and especially for anyone who is protected by the corporate perception filter that many middle-class men enjoy, which immunises them from the suspicion of *actually* being an idiot; it's brilliant. Nonetheless, honesty about what we don't know or fully understand at work, coupled with unfettered curiosity, is valuable – even as it can make us feel vulnerable. I think Molly Graham and I also disagree on the reality of 'stupid questions' and on a scripting point for being vulnerable when you don't understand.

She suggests that it's OK to say, 'This might be a stupid question. . .' or 'Sorry if this is a dumb question, but. . .' before you ask your question, but I think this *informs* the listener that this *is* a stupid question.

I don't think the preponderance of people with power in meeting rooms are kind or empathetic enough to understand that you're actually asking an important question that may seem simple. Instead, I prefer precursor elements like, 'I'd like to clarify. . .' or 'I want to ensure I've understood completely. . .' – at least this way, the implication that I am less competent has to be generated by their own minds, rather than taken from my own words!

Notwithstanding the myths about vulnerability's utility, it's a route to performance enhancement. Used effectively, it can *humanise leaders*[2] and enable stronger connections with colleagues, encourage *psychological safety*[3] and *open communication,*[4] encourage *innovation and creativity*[5] and increase *motivation and engagement*[6] as I'll talk about later; it is a simple way to empower others when employed legitimately.

In this chapter, I hope to encourage you to show vulnerability as a personal and team performance enhancer and share how to be vulnerable effectively to avoid some of the anxieties you may feel about it, which may be holding you back.

Vulnerability isn't complex to demonstrate, even as its rarity in practice suggests so. It can be as simple as a person as a leader or a well-thought-of person in a group acknowledging a mistake without being prompted or cajoled.

Asking for help demonstrates vulnerability, like showing limitations in your knowledge or capacity. Even sharing minor aspects of your life outside of work is vulnerable in a world where you might be considered solely in the context of your role or title.

So why do so many leaders find it so difficult?

FUNCTIONAL VULNERABILITY

When I talk to leaders about *functional vulnerability*, many instantly think I am suggesting a 'leader bares all' competition where they are stripped of their assets and left a broken, naked shadow of their authentic selves in front of their teams.

This occurs because the myth of vulnerability as an ON/OFF switch is pervasive: you either share every deficit or challenge area or nothing at all.

Leaders fear that when they share vulnerabilities, they will lose credibility, but the opposite is true. A Kellogg School of Management study indicates that people 'prefer to work for people who can make themselves vulnerable'. Indeed, that same study found that 'leaders who confess faults are seen as more authentic but no less competent than those who don't, and that employees prefer to work with leaders who admit their foibles'.

I would suggest to you, as valuable as this kind of research is – and as much as I love (and embody) words like 'foible' – words like 'admit' and 'confess' only hinder disclosure and authentic vulnerability. Where disclosure is simply valuable and personally significant, 'sharing' is the word I use, and where a colleague or leader talks about a mistake they've made, 'acknowledge' is good enough for me, especially when accompanied by the correct amount of contrition and a commitment not to repeat their mistake.

When the goal is to inspire the performance and empowerment of your team, vulnerability is best shared when it's well-curated, contextually valuable, and the group has earned the disclosure through its consistent approach to psychological safety.

Let's discuss those aspects one at a time.

Well-Curated

In most organisational environments, it's vital that vulnerability disclosures be reasoned and considered, not a knee-jerk response to external stimuli. This means considering how to approach sharing your vulnerabilities, that is:

- *Measured*: enough information to grant insight to others but not so much as to overwhelm, bearing in mind, as I'll discuss later, that the amount of information you can share without overwhelming someone grows over time with the strength and authenticity of the relationships concerned.

- *Objective*: delivered in a way that doesn't over or under-emphasise the importance or impact of what's being shared – avoiding hyperbole or the 'slippery slope' narrative.
- *Appropriate*: not everything you have is relevant to share in every environment and it is undoubtedly true that sharing a deeply personal moral failing with your team members is more likely to inspire contempt – with a desire for your team to escape to another leader – than the authenticity you were looking for.

Contextually Valuable

Not everything we think to share is valuable in every moment or context, and some thought about why we are sharing is important for that sharing to be seen as authentic rather than transparently manipulative. Sadly, many of us have experienced people who share something personal in an attempt to justify their missteps. I went to grad school with one student who had two different pets die during two different missed exams.

I think the following framework is simplistic, but it provides additional guidance for those concerned about the impact of showing vulnerability at work. If we were to split contextual vulnerabilities into three arbitrary categories – technical, strategic and personal – then we might consider some examples:

- o *Technical*: Sharing specific gaps or deficits in your knowledge with an additional request for support in these specific areas when you suspect others in your team have insights or expertise they have not yet voiced.

- *Strategic*: Stating where you are concerned about your ability to thoroughly scrutinise or judge a project or strategic plan because of your blind spots, a particular perspective or fixed-mindset thinking. You might share your concern, asking for others to 'play devil's advocate' or share views from other perspectives, even if they aren't their own.

- *Personal*: Sharing that you are a human in an environment where others may know you transactionally or have a sense of your omniscience and invulnerability because of your track record of success. This may mean measured, objective and appropriate sharing of small, simple humanising personal factors. I might share my love of Star Wars, e-bikes, and beach holidays, allowing easy entry into a more human space without the significant threat of interpersonal friction.

Earned Disclosure

People earn the right to know things about you that may be vulnerable. This goes beyond the technical disclosure I wrote about earlier, where colleagues owe it to their teams to acknowledge, disclose and own their technical mistakes; we disclose when it feels earned.

Lots of small behaviours encourage this.

- *Empathy and respect*: Queer people who hadn't previously shared their sexuality in the workplace often speak about listening to their straight colleagues speaking kindly about LGBTQ+ issues or stories or using language that includes their community as a reason they choose to share their sexuality, saying 'they earned the right to know'.

- *Reciprocal disclosure*: Where all colleagues know that learning about others is contingent on being willing to share about themselves. Where people can indicate their curiosity for others by sharing small things about themselves in the hope that this will be reciprocated up to, and not beyond any personal boundaries for any party.

- *Respecting boundaries*: Even when a person is appropriately curious about another, or someone is willing to share something, further disclosure can be curtailed because of the expectation of ever more disclosure, despite obvious reluctance. When the point of reluctance to share more is reached, gratitude and not frustration are the answer.

- *Genuine interest and cognitive engagement*: Too many people ask a question – even intimate questions – of colleagues and then proceed to check out mentally; eyes glaze over, they glance at their phone or look off into the distance – we'll talk more about authentic listening later in the book – but this disengagement means future disclosure is far less likely. My guiding principle is: 'Don't ask if you don't care'.

- *Service versus selfish curiosity*: A simple guide – if you ever interrogate why you want to know something, it can reveal whether it will be a positive interaction. If you ask yourself, 'Why am I asking this?' and the answer is 'Because'. Or 'I just want to know', then you are likely getting yourself into a space where you'll be seen to impose or over-impose on your colleague.

Asking the details of someone's disability to ensure the team day you are organising will be accessible feels a lot different than asking because you didn't know.

I get asked about my height about 20 times a week, and it's dull, mainly because the people who ask don't care. It's obvious. I was big, and they were surprised to see me in their shop, street or pub and just had to say something.

I have not once had a relationship blossom with someone who introduced themselves with a question about my height.

Just so you know.

Phatic Expressions

When considering these best practice criteria, I want to introduce you to the term 'phatic expression' – something I learned from TikTok a few years ago and then went down a rabbit hole with it for months! A 'phatic expression' is a type of communication that serves a social function rather than conveying information or meaning. These expressions are used to establish or maintain social contact, acknowledge another person's presence, or manage the flow of conversation. It's not just 'small talk'; it's the exchange we have where we avoid overly literal, overly detailed or 'brutally' honest insights or responses before a mutually strong social connection and understanding has developed.

I am not telling you that vulnerability at work *only* serves a social function, but how our phatic expressions – perhaps our greetings with people who have become close colleagues – are a good way to measure the natural growth and development of your non-technical vulnerability disclosures. You may have started with a curt 'How are you?' on entering the office, with a 'just fine' in return, but a year later, you've developed that phatic norm with your work bestie into something deeper and more personalised, so much so that if either party returns to the initial 'How are you? – fine!' ritual, you think something is very wrong.

So, for vulnerability, we start with the convention of avoiding 'aphatic utterances' that overshare, are over-long and are overwhelming.

I think of leaders' vulnerability from the perspective of the artform of burlesque. It starts off with slow measured reveals that don't overwhelm, but creates engagement and anticipation for more fulsome sharing when the time is right.

Where leaders' vulnerability is concerned, be transparent, but pace yourself.

EMPOWERING YOUR TEAMS

There are so many opportunities to use vulnerability to empower your teams and those around you. Out of necessity, I am, among other kinds, a 'contextual leader'. I am simply in too many environments where I don't know everything to take the lead in every moment. More than that, even if I could blag my expertise, I'd miss an opportunity with the group I led. It is vital to clearly (granularly and objectively) state where you are less knowledgeable or informed than others on the team and proactively elevate them to lead in specific contexts where their expertise supersedes yours. Empowerment comes from acknowledging where you are not *the* best equipped – and inviting others to lead in those spaces. This is not an abdication of authority but an amplification of team insight. It's not an attempt to paint (or reveal) yourself a floundering imbecile but rather an opportunity for a nuanced examination of relative expertise in context.

I was once invited into a writers' room for a big Hollywood studio, and I saw a really great leader who wanted to engage and receive contributions from everyone in that room. However, they suffered from no one believing they didn't already know everything because they weren't ever explicit about what they didn't know (and in the absence of that, their successful studio was a proxy for their unassailable brilliance). Additionally, the invitation to contribute – to lead contextually – was daunting: 'Does anyone else have any thoughts?' was often said in the waning minutes of a creative agenda item.

This environment is not where a callous leader tries to quiet or intimidate, but the result is the same. It would be a brave colleague who spoke at all in that situation after sager voices had spoken so much.

Remember that this contextual leadership, with explicit permission to drive an agenda item or an area of expertise, doesn't change final decision-making authority, but the expertise you invite and your recognition of its superiority over yours mean you weigh their contribution more heavily in your decision-making formula.

Next, we come to credit; in the research my team and I have done, being recognised for good ideas, questions and contributions is right up there in the list of contemporary expectations of leaders.

You will never read or hear me take something brilliant I say that has been learned from others or is the product of another researcher's work without reference to that person or a full citation. Beyond having experienced this myself and not wanting to do it to others, stealing others' original thoughts diminishes personal credibility, and not just within academia.

Crediting in this way is a form of practical vulnerability. You know full well what it sounds like when leaders take other people's words for their own; those leaders you've had who say, 'As I always say...' before adding a well-known business cliché, that they want you to suspend belief and accept it as their unique thought. These people do not rise in our estimation. One of the many consequences of this behaviour is it convinces the people around the perpetrators that they will steal and take as their own every original thought you ever have – ensuring you will be more guarded and less open in any conversation, meeting or email chain in which they are present.

Crediting is not just about great quotes and research; it's also about ensuring that the people who germinate ideas or contribute in some way to outcomes around you are proactively connected to those outcomes.

We all know that the less senior a person is, the more likely their work will be mundane, despite being entirely vital for more significant strategic outcomes that senior colleagues 'own'.

I think it's our job, especially leaders or other people with seniority in organisations, to connect contributors at every level to the outcomes that people notice. Some may question if this is indeed a form of vulnerability, but my experience watching how difficult – almost painful at times – it is for so many senior people to grant some small piece of credit for an outcome to a more junior cohort doing meaningful but onerous work tells me it *must* make them feel vulnerable in some way to want to avoid sharing the credit so much.

Lastly, one of the most fulfilling and effective ways to be vulnerable is by sharing the 'secret sauce' of things you do that others see as 'magic' – giving them a detailed description of where you learned it, a set of step-by-step instructions, helping them to be able to emulate your success. It is vulnerable indeed to attempt to describe elements of your expertise that others see as uniquely brilliant and perhaps innate. However, as I've mentioned previously, gatekeeping, simply to allow the mysticism to remain about your capabilities, is short-sighted in any world where sustainable success is a team game. One that requires a succession plan!

Perhaps the most challenging thing for accomplished people is that vulnerability requires a granularity of insight and a confident self-assurance that sometimes reveals to you more than you'd prefer to examine in detail.

I've had this 'vulnerability coaching conversation' with senior leaders around the world, and whether in the Middle East, Asia, Europe or North America, I have seen the resistance and listened as they talk around the uncomfortable – and instead of leaning into introspection, they fabricate a vulnerability.

Vulnerability can't be manufactured – don't pretend you have a gap, deficiency or challenge where there is none. It's inauthentic in the extreme and will appear to others as manipulative and trust-toxic. Pretending you need help where you don't is short-sighted from a performance and empowerment perspective and can actually lead to frustration. It usually leads to you pretending you don't know in an area you do and forcing others, who may well know less, to guess.

A global software company I worked with had a senior leader who, in an attempt to be 'collaborative, engaging and empowering', asked open questions to which they already knew the answers. Far from creating the knitted team they'd hoped, it allowed an energetic undercurrent of frustration to build and in 360 conversations with direct reports, the ask was clear: 'Just tell me when you know the answer . . . and let me shine when I know more than you!'

Vulnerability is not helplessness; it isn't inauthentic to curate how you present doubt and gaps in knowledge to your team. Doubt, fear and anxiety can all be genuinely conveyed as long as they are objective and specific rather than hyperbolic and holistic. For example, share how you are objectively concerned about a particular element of a plan instead of conveying a general lack of faith in the overall strategy. Share the fact that you experience performance anxiety in particular. You can educate your team that some kinds of anxiety should be normalised as it is a key component of preparation for high performance and, indeed, what guards against taking familiar challenges for granted.

Similarly, should you have moments where you experience imposter phenomena, sharing those can be empowering to a team of people who may regard 'someone like you' as immune, and that can help put their own self-doubt into context.

In *The Promises of Giants*, I wrote that leaders who present as invulnerable often attract sycophants, not teammates, which can lead to brittle decisions and poor crisis performance.

As you balance the effort you might be willing to make to become authentically, pragmatically and effectively vulnerable with your team and peers, please remember the image of the solitary Great White shark swimming through the deep blue, covered at all times by a collection of remoras, making no contribution – just adding drag and causing occasional skin irritation. True vulnerability attracts contributors, not hangers on.

As I consider the effort required to empower a collection into a team, I find that image motivating.

Principles into Practice: Making it Real
Exercises to Practise Vulnerability as a Leadership Asset

1. Reframe the Ask
- Consider an actual request or clarification you need.
- Write it in three ways:
    a) raw/insecure
    b) overly deferential
    c) professionally vulnerable (using the guidance from this chapter).
- Use the third version in your next meeting or email.

2. Clarify Without Apology
- Think about the common phrases you might use, like 'Sorry if this is dumb. . .' or 'This might be a stupid question. . .'

- Take these more neutral examples 'to ensure clarity. . .' or 'can you expand on. . .' and create more examples in your own voice.
- Practise using these neutral phrases in your meetings.
- Reflect on any change in response or tone from colleagues.

3. Credit Publicly

- At the end of each week, identify one idea, phrase or insight you used that came from someone else.
- Credit them publicly (email, meeting, message).
- Log how it affects your team's openness and sense of recognition.

4. Vulnerability Mapping

- Identify three current work challenges.
- For each, mark:
  a) Where am I uncertain?
  b) Who might know more than me?
  c) What framing could I use to invite their input without diminishing my role?

5. Reveal, Don't Collapse

- Think of a past instance when you expressed anxiety or doubt.
- Rewrite it now more objectively and specifically, preserving honesty while protecting leadership presence.

6. Curated Confidence Journal

- Keep a weekly log of moments where you revealed a vulnerability and what resulted.
- Did people engage more, trust more and open up in return?
- What was the impact on your credibility?

CHAPTER SIX

EXCELLENCE IN COMMUNICATION

IT'S NOT MAGIC. . . IT'S ELOQUENCE

DEFINING ELOQUENCE

I understand that when I say eloquence, people will naturally fall prey to the nationalistic and somewhat colonial perspectives on eloquence. I am not talking about regional or other accents or speech impediments. Having travelled the world and been the long-standing vice-president of an amazing disability charity, The Activity Alliance, I have had way enough experience with both scenarios to realise that often the inability to understand someone else in those circumstances has as much to do with their personal resentment at having to put *any* effort into the mutuality of effective communication and a personal bias against people who don't communicate like they do.

Don't be fooled by people with British RP ('Received Pronunciation' – think how the Royal Family sounds or old BBC news broadcasts from the 1950s), or the other 'acceptable' regional accents from whatever region you live, or those people who use flowery, overly elaborate and often anachronistic language that emphasises aesthetics or status over effectiveness. True eloquence in speech and word is precision and intentionality in communication, not ornamentation.

I was really proud of that description until I realised that I'd just described myself (at least some of the time!)

More simply put, and the definition you'll hear from me if you ever listen to one of my speeches, is 'eloquence is the ability to transfer your ideas, information, feelings and intent from your mind to that of another, with the least chance of misinterpretation'.

Eloquence is a form of generosity in communication that provides clarity, insight and understanding to others. It requires effort – and not just in choosing precisely the right kind and number of words to use in any exchange but also in understanding your audience, be it a single person or a conference hall full of thousands, to know how to tailor your engagement.

The evidence is clear: eloquence in leaders correlates with perceived leadership credibility. Clarity and conciseness are also linked to higher trustworthiness[1] and influence in organisational contexts.[2]

PRECISION IN COMMUNICATION

Eloquent communication begins in the mind, and I have been clear that where poor behaviour and even cruel or clumsy language is concerned, not 'meaning' to insult or degrade is no extenuating circumstance. This doesn't change the fact that the best way to begin elevating your ability to communicate effectively is to sharpen your thoughts before expression – clarity begins in self-reflection by asking yourself questions like:

- What, specifically, do you want your audience to know?
- How do you want them to feel after hearing you speak?
- What do you want them (to be motivated) to do?

For that last parenthetical part, you may be one of those people who always has the luxury of talking to groups of people who always *have* to do as you tell them, but as a psychologist, educator, consultant, speaker and coach, I don't   I can only choose the right words, delivered most clearly and appropriately for the audience concerned, and *hope* I have stimulated them to act on the ideas or suggestions I have laid out.

Eloquence requires active decision-making about words, tone and pacing, and I'll discuss each of these factors in more detail.

Use Your Words

When you consider your audience, your work level, the experience of your audience and their general level of formal academic qualifications (again, with almost no bearing on their actual intelligence and intellectual curiosity), you can target the kinds of words and phrases (including the use of specialist acronyms and technical terms.

You can use many readability scales, most built into word processor programmes. I use whatever is built in, with my judgement added, given that I may use a lot of acronyms that are second nature to clients or academics, but might change the readability score without that context.

The index I like a lot – primarily because of the name – is the UK adaptation of the SMOG readability index, created by psychologist G. Harry McLaughlin in 1969. That is, *The Simplified Measure of Gobbledygook* (SMOG) – a simply brilliant name and acronym I first heard about while working in the NHS in Manchester.

It looks at the multisyllabic words in a text sample (3+ syllables), runs them through an algorithm and spits out a score. Professional writing should have a SMOG score of 10–12, which aligns (roughly) with the period of studying for and taking A-levels in the United Kingdom or the 10–12th grade in the United States.

There is an organisation in the United Kingdom called the Plain English Campaign – whose work I really respect, even as I think they'd like to give me a good talking to from time to time – who generally advises that even for professional audiences, keeping readability scores lower than might be expected often improves engagement and retention of information. This is especially worth considering when the news you are sharing will likely emotionally impact your audience or workforce.

Both the Plain English Campaign[3] and the National Literacy Trust,[4] an organisation I used to be an ambassador for, often cite SMOG or the Gunning Fog Index,[5] which has a website where you can insert your text and get a readability score as key methods of ensuring accessibility of writing, whether it's going to be read by others alone, or by you to others.

I just entered what I've written for this chapter into the Gunning Fog Index website and got a score of 19.5. Given that score, my editors have quite a job; it's a score reserved for academic papers and legal documents. I appreciate the extra effort if you're still with me and enjoying this – I really do!

If you are a fellow nerd and would like to read up on the options and even see the algorithms behind the various readability scores, you can try the website from 'Readable'.[6]

Tone

Almost everyone can moderate and reorient their tone for an audience. You see little children do it when asking for something they know they shouldn't be asking for – whether it's ice cream for dinner or staying up past their bedtime. At work, we have recognised where we need someone's support but have no right or power to demand it, and we instinctively know the 'professional but pleading' tone in our voice. Every British person seems to have the ability to use the word 'fine' to mean everything from 'That's great, thank you!' to 'You have disappointed me to the point of disownment; you best hope we never meet again'.

In my sessions on becoming a more eloquent speaker, I tell audiences that our inability to get the tone right combines several points. None of them is particularly flattering.

1. They don't understand the audience or how they or their perceptions may require a targeted tone.
2. They don't care about the audience enough to care about the impact of a mis-toned communication.
3. They don't think the audience is important or influential enough to worry about their perception.

They sound rough, but I'd ask you to consider some famous communication blunders. These are often scripted words that go through tens of experts' hands before being spoken, so how do they end up being so wildly wrong? – from former BP boss Tony Hayward, who said, 'I'd like my life back', in the middle of an environmental catastrophe that had claimed colleagues' lives, to Ellen DeGeneres comparing quarantine in her mansion to 'being in jail' during early COVID-19 lockdowns. Please don't think that it's just spontaneous gaffes – a *lot* of people were involved when Steve Jobs told all of us iPhone owners, with a tone the equivalent of a verbal eye-roll, that the antenna was just fine and instead, we were 'holding it wrong'.

Pacing

I speak incredibly slowly.

It's the same whether addressing a conference hall or a coaching client.

I didn't know that I spoke especially slowly until our social media team told me how they edit hours of silent space from many of the videos you may see on LinkedIn, Instagram, TickTok or BlueSky.

I don't know what made me speak slowly, although I suspect it has to do with my extra senior year in high school in Toledo, Ohio. I arrived in the middle of the summer, prepared for pre-season, and I was met off the plane by my new coach, who had a warm smile and a face wrinkled – I suspect – by thousands of preventable on-court mistakes by players over the decades.

He shook my hand and spoke, and only then did I realise that Americans don't speak English.

I spent the first month nodding and smiling at people from the great state of Ohio, who, with all the best will in the world, I broadly didn't understand.

I'd ask for water and get orange juice, or 'tea' and get 'pop'; before quickly realising if I wanted anything I asked for, I'd need to slow down and enunciate!

One of the advantages of my slow speech – bearing in mind not everyone can pull this off – feeds into the myth of spontaneity – the idea that some people have the 'gift of the gab'. The truth is that most spontaneous brilliance is *rehearsed authenticity*.

A good example is my favourite kind of speech – what we call a fireside chat – where I am asked questions in front of a camera or an audience by a senior stakeholder in a company or a more junior stakeholder who's being rewarded for their outstanding work. I never see the questions beforehand; I am just told about the themes I will address. I am categorically worse at providing compelling answers if my brain has a chance to workshop and re-rehearse a potential response. This has nothing to do with my 'soaring' intellect or my ability to be spontaneous and more to do with 'recombinative creativity', my ability to draw from the library of experiences I talked about in Chapter 3 and extrapolate aspects of old solutions to new but related contexts and provide plausible (although not always correct) responses. In addition, though, there is the fact that I spend a *lot* of time thinking about what I might be asked in response to the things I say or am likely to say.

Of course, I am concerned with argumentative rebuttals. However, I am even more interested in people inspired to ask clarifying questions or understand how my statements or ideas relate to their particular situation. As such, there is a background process that occurs as I think about an audience I've researched that includes:

1. What context or information have I omitted for brevity that could leave the audience with questions?
2. What context do I have in my mind while creating this content, and how might I need to change this for them?
3. What's the most obvious evidence-based challenge to my assertions; do I have my evidence and reasoning ready?
4. What's the most obvious contrarian or 'bad-faith' challenge to my assertions; do I have a reasoned response?

This chapter features many of my favourites. I love speaking to people, sharing ideas and learning from the audience. And I love teaching people – especially those who've been told because of some quirk of personality or birth that they will never be compelling – how they can communicate (and tell stories) more effectively.

When constructed carefully and spoken sincerely, they become poignant to the point of appearing mystical. When I read fantasy books as a kid, it always struck me that monarchs and warriors (invariably men) would be rewarded for rousing speeches that uplift armies or whole kingdoms. However, women who used words that moved people were invariably called witches; their words called 'spells' and prospects diminished for it.

I've known that words have real power since I was seven years old, listening to my mother, a family doctor, calm and support the families of sick and dying patients and soothe exhausted colleagues.

STORYTELLING

One mechanism for eloquence is storytelling. As a species, we have communicated what's important, from the threat of wild beasts to our understanding of our origins through storytelling. We've been sharing stories since our primitive relatives chewed berries and sprayed the juice on their hands to create cave art depicting their lives. It remains one of the most powerful communication tools available to us.

There is a story for every situation. I don't know that I've ever been so certain about anything I say. There is a story for every moment we face, whether alone, within our family or with our work teams.

To steal from Isaac Asimov, who spoke about the importance of science fiction (something I believe with conviction!):

> 'Individual science fiction stories may seem as trivial as ever to the blinder critics and philosophers of today, but the core of science fiction, its essence, has become crucial to our salvation if we are to be saved at all'.[7]

But I believe we can simplify and use this quote just for stories and storytelling:

> Individual stories may seem trivial to today's myopic critics and philosophers, but storytelling's core, its essence, is crucial to our salvation.

Asimov knew that science fiction stories could facilitate time travel, but all storytelling is time travel.

When you tell a story well, people think the past or the future (depending on the nature of the story) spills from the words and washes over the audience. But no, great storytelling is much more potent than that. Great storytelling picks the reader or the audience up and takes them instantaneously forward or back in time. As you describe, they see the world through your or the author's eyes; as you share how you feel, they feel it too, vividly and real as if happening to them, and as you finish, as if by magic, they emerge back to this moment – but in their brains is a story that feels more like a memory.

The aim of great storytelling is an intimate, non-exploitative relationship that gives access and perspective that might not be achieved otherwise. When complete, it creates a set of shared emotional time-stamps, the present moment and the time where the story originated.

I'm not going to talk too much about reading actual stories, although a lot of what I'll share next might apply. It's more about telling stories that use memories and moments to illustrate points.

Tools of Storytelling
Recall the Moment with Fidelity

Including 'insignificant' sensory details or aspects of the memory that seem unrelated to the point you want to make helps the story to feel more real.

There is a reason that all the real-to-life TV shows and films you watch have other cars on the road, whether parked or driving, when showing you a protagonist's conversation in a car. If they didn't, eventually, you would be yanked out of the story because your mind keeps telling you that something is wrong and missing, which won't allow you to focus on the protagonist – 'Why aren't there any other cars on the road?!' In this way, and in carefully measured amounts, adding what might otherwise be considered noise or distraction to a story counterintuitively helps your audience focus on what you want them to see.

How many of these details can you add is a balance – too many and your story will lose integrity (and last too long), too few and the story lacks authenticity. I recommend that for any story of consequence you might think about sharing, there will be moments you think of as small but meaningful to you only because you were there, but those 'inside references' are the ideal details to add. Pick one, or maybe two, peppered into your story to add that little something special.

These details don't have to be central to the story. I tell a story about where my love of *Star Wars* began, and describe watching my mother reach for our shared box of popcorn as we watched *A New Hope* – a nugget of information I first added on a self-indulgent whim 30 years ago – and I still remember being awestruck by the difference it made for the audience.

Offer Inner Monologue

Share what you were thinking or feeling when recalling something from the past in a granular and vivid way. For stories about the future, including those you tell to illustrate a shared goal, vision or mission, ensure you incorporate some detail on the positive emotions or prescient concerns you might expect to feel, especially if there will be initial hardship during the struggle to achieve that shared goal.

Invoking emotion is a key aspect of storytelling's power – the emotion conveyed by the storyteller and that inspired or resonated with the listeners. Stories that engage emotion and sensory detail activate the same neural pathways as lived experience in listeners.[8] So by engaging emotion, you can turn a story into something that imprints like a personal experience.[9]

Inhabit the Moment

I don't tell stories by looking at memories and reading from them like a book. I live there. I dip back into the memory and re-experience it to spot the extra details I might share and authentically convey the emotions from that moment.

This again is not some superpower of mine – you do it all the time! You have certainly spontaneously shuddered when a cringeworthy moment resurfaced in your mind, or laughed out loud as a memory reinstalled itself in your present moment. Some of the most amazing moments we have with loved ones are when we all inhabit the exact same moment, whether laughing or crying; it is bonding to be of one mind, living in a moment, like (actually good) virtual reality, seeing each other in that space, transported in time.

One helpful tip for this immersion is to set up the story with as little detail as possible – don't preamble for 10 minutes to set up a 3-minute story, find a sentence that works as an introduction, and it can be as banal as you like – no one will remember the setup. For my introduction to the *Star Wars* story I mentioned, one of my setups is: 'I remember when I knew I would become a psychologist. . .' Once the preamble is done, switch to speaking in the present tense to heighten immersion. Once you get good at this fundamental engagement, you can then play with time travel, pulling people into the past with a story, bringing them back to observe what's shared, and then diving back into the past.

Know If You Are a Comedian

I am not. I remember the first time an audience laughed in unison at something I said in a presentation at a conference. And I remember being confused – it had not been a prepared line! I think the difference between being able to occasionally make people laugh and being a comedian is whether you tell jokes. One of the worst advice for speakers is to start with a joke. Not only does this often lead to offence if you don't *really* know the audience and they *really* understand you, but they often fall flat and reek of inexperienced or formulaic speakers.

Do not perform *for* laughs, but let authentic emotion surface freely, and if something was or is funny to you in some moment past or present, that will be experienced by your audience.

Structure and Pacing – The Plane Journey Metaphor

If I have coached you, you will at some point hear me ask you to 'land the plane!' This is part of what I think is a useful and elegant metaphor to structure how stories should be crafted and delivered.

Boarding

Start with *immediate inclusion*. It is essential that everyone feels like they're in the privileged 'boarding group 1'. No one wants to sit at the boarding gate watching other people 'get on board' while they stare at their ticket, wondering why everyone else is so special that they get seated early. Equally, the process of boarding the plane has got to be well explained or straightforward because no one wants to feel willing to board and then realise they're missing something essential just as they get to the threshold.

Pushback and Taxi

Once people are on board, keep it brief. I don't know anyone who flies regularly – and remember that everyone listening to you tell a story is a seasoned listener to stories – who wants to linger listening to breathy and consistently muffled captains explain the route. If you need to contextualise or familiarise the audience with a potentially unfamiliar storytelling equipment, contextualise efficiently and briefly, or failing that, take a lesson from Southwest Airlines and make it wacky. I don't have the chops for wacky, so I stick to concise.

Take-off

Create narrative momentum. Audiences don't mind a little scene-setting, but they do need to feel the 'thrust' when the story becomes emotionally or intellectually engaging pretty early on. I have been to enough major airport hubs to know how frustrating it is to drive, seemingly endlessly, around them in an Airbus 380, and the subsequent relief when I finally feel that the plane is going somewhere as the engines roar.

Cruising Altitude

This is where you can develop the body of the story. Introduce richness, and those human, seemingly minor details that enhance the experience. It's worth remembering that this is the place for turbulence ('conflict'). It's where it's expected and where it can, if not measured, disrupt the flow, like when your beverage arrives and you're settling in, and then turbulence leaves you wearing your drink. Some storytellers say that this is what people want – I am yet to enjoy that experience metaphorically or actually.

The journey matters more than the twist or critical tension. While people can leave flights talking about the turbulence, that's usually considered a bad flight! Tension and conflict are ways of engaging listeners in stories, but especially now in our conflict-ridden, transformation-heavy, VUCA (volatility, uncertainty, complexity, and ambiguity) world, there is a place for stories that have predictable justice. Where it is clear to your passengers that, despite any turbulence, everything will be OK.

Audiences often prefer these assured outcomes over twist endings.

I have curated how I get the news nowadays in part because otherwise, the world's tribulations negatively affect my mood and my ability to be a proactive agent of change in this world.

I *am* still paying attention, and anyone who knows me knows I have strong views and have taken decisive actions on lots of issues, but I psychologically spiral with too many stories of hate, pain and destruction in my media feeds. That's why I have taken some refuge in Agatha Christie and their descendants' detective shows like Poirot and Columbo. Perhaps a reason why they endure is that we're comforted by the protagonist's inevitable success. I have seen every episode of all those series. Still, on a Sunday, if I'm not travelling, writing or working, I will be waiting to hear Columbo ask 'just one more thing' or Poirot give that knowing look, so I can relax knowing 10 minutes into this 60-minute programme, the killer is as good as caught.

Stories (and indeed most communication) aren't just about the destination, especially in corporate and familial communication: the outcome is often known or designated, but the story explains *why* this particular destination matters in a way that each person can connect to from their own perspective.

Land the Plane

Knowing you are close to your destination creates urgency. People listening to you want the payoff. Equally, as keen as people are to get back on the ground, no one wants to feel like they are careening out of the sky out of control or dropping like a stone with an abrupt thud. Instead, people want to feel their approach is controlled and direct, without the inexorable, seemingly inevitable and frustrating holding loops around their obvious destination.

Bring the story to a conclusion with unhurried, but steady pacing, and once your wheels touch, finish.

So many speakers don't know when to end so they keep talking, hoping for the perfect last line, and in doing so, lose the audience who are already unbuckled, arms tensed on their armrest, eyeing the luggage bin they *hope* they put their carry-on in, while staring at the fasten seatbelt sign so they can bolt to the exit the moment it *pings*.

Don't make people wait too long for their *ping*.

I know that it can be hard to understand how to end a story, but I implore you not to use the plaintive, 'That's it', 'So, yeah. . .', 'I guess that's all,' or 'Thank you for listening. . .' and instead use pace, tone, silence and presence to send the message, ironically, loud and clear.

Slow your cadence, embrace your audience with your attention, and bring everyone back to now, from wherever they were, back to the seat, the room and the time they're sitting in, right now.

Breathe more slowly and purposefully as you conclude, and allow them to emerge as if from a shared meditation as much as a shared memory, forever changed by the experience.

By all means, remind them of any short messages you want to reinforce from your comments, then – without remorse or delay – land the plane.

ELOQUENCE IS EVERYDAY POWER

Effective communication is the act of intentionally creating meaning for others. Some call it 'more art than science' and, by implication, suggest it's something not all of us can master. By that definition, it's *still* part science, and it's undoubtedly a discipline.

It's the synthesis of what you mean to convey, the discipline and care with which you shape your words and presentation, and a deep empathy for how this combination may land differently, with different people, in different moments.

In a world of noise, eloquence is rare – and therefore powerful. It's a power we can all wield, because it's a skill: Eloquence is built, not bestowed.

Practice into Practice: Making it Real

Here are some tools I use to remain sharp and improve.

Activity: Record Yourself as a Speaker/Storyteller

Video 1: Record yourself telling a 3–5 minute meaningful story or anecdote to yourself, one you don't need a script to recount.

Deliver it to camera with no audience. Don't rehearse it; tell it while looking towards the camera.

Do not initially watch this recording before completing the next step.

Find one or more family members, friends or close colleagues and ask them to join a meeting on a recordable video meeting platform.

Video 2: Record the same 3–5 minute story again, this time with an audience.

Ask your listeners to stay silent, not interrupt, but otherwise act with the usual meeting decorum. Set your video to 'pinned' or the setting that enlarges the speaker's video.

Don't forget to let them know you'll record this and that you won't broadcast it!

First, watch video 1 with the sound off. Eloquence includes awareness of non-verbal context and ambient communication – your audience is always listening, even in silence.

As you watch the silent video, pay attention to the following aspects:

- Facial expressions
  - Are they congruent with your message?
  - Do you look emotionally engaged or detached?
  - Do your expressions fluctuate meaningfully, or are you static?
  - Do you smile?

(Continued)

- Gestures and hand movements
  - Do your hands support the story, or are they distracting or repetitive?
  - Are gestures purposeful, or do they look nervous (e.g., fiddling, rubbing hands, arms permanently crossed)?
- Posture and stance
  - Do you appear grounded, confident, stiff, slouched, fidgety or something else?
  - Is your body oriented with the audience or camera, or do you seem closed off?
- Movement and physical space
  - Do you use the space meaningfully, e.g., moving during transitions or staying still for emphasis?
  - Are you pacing aimlessly, or standing still like you're bolted to the floor?
- Eye contact (if facing the camera or audience)
  - Are you scanning the audience consciously or darting your eyes nervously?
  - Do you connect with the camera or avoid it altogether?
- Pacing and rhythm (visually)
  - Is there visual rhythm in your delivery – pauses, beats, stillness – or is it a visual blur?

Then watch yourself on video 2, with the sound off, and respond to these same questions.

Reflect on whether some of the challenges, deficits or highlights you saw without an audience are now less or more noticeable.

If your audience's faces are visible, look a third time at this video and consider the following factors and whether they evolve over the length of the video:

- Eye contact – Are they looking at you or elsewhere (emails on screen or other colleagues)?
- Mirroring behaviours – Do they unconsciously mirror your gestures or postures?
- Facial responsiveness – Are there visible signs of emotion that match the moment?
- Body orientation – Are their bodies, not just their heads, turned towards you?
- Focus and stillness – Is there minimal fidgeting and a notable focus on you? Do listeners lean forward when you emphasise key ideas?

Then watch videos 1 and 2 back to back with the sound on. What differences do you notice from the no-audio versions?

Are some of the challenges, deficits or highlights you saw without audio now less or more noticeable?

Now you can hear yourself as well as see yourself, consider:

- Tone and modulation
  - Are you using variation in tone to signal energy, emotion, or shifts in the story?
  - Do you sound natural, or is your delivery monotone, overly performative, or robotic?
- Pacing and pauses
  - Do you rush, or give ideas time to land?
  - Are you breathing intentionally, or talking until breathless?

(Continued)

123

- Clarity and articulation
  - Are you enunciating, or are words slurring or mumbling?
  - Can the audience easily follow your key points?
- Emphasis and rhythm
  - Are you highlighting key words and phrases?
  - Do you repeat for effect or structure, or ramble?
- Emotional congruence
  - Does your tone match your story?
  - Do you sound as moved or amused as you look?
- Message and story arc
  - Is the story clear and compelling?
  - Are you building towards a payoff or insight, or meandering?
  - Do you 'land the plane?'

You can play with this format if you want to dive deeper and do things like:

- Play back audio only – Does the meaning hold or change without seeing yourself?
- Read a children's book – Record yourself reading it aloud as if to children attending a library reading of their favourite book. You'll find this a test of clarity, tone variation, and engagement and a lesson to debunk the idea that you can't change your tone to suit your audience!

CHAPTER SEVEN

TRANSFORMING PERCEIVED WEAKNESSES

IT'S NOT MAGIC. . . IT'S EVOLUTION

Everyone has flaws. Call them personal challenges or glaring gaps – they are real and universal.

People approach these gaps on a spectrum. The archetypes I describe next might be familiar to you – they might even be you – but these aren't judgements, and, as I said, where our weaknesses are concerned, we're on a spectrum.

I've met some people – leaders in industry and public service – who've clearly decided that the only way for them to be effective and functional in this society is to have one supreme skill that they are exempt even from speculation about their need for personal growth.

Others I have met don't necessarily think they are supreme at anything, but consider themselves so roundly competent that it would be churlish for anyone else to point out an area for development. Secretly, they suspect it would be devastating if they personally acknowledged any truth in feedback that threatened to illuminate their well-cultivated blind spot.

Then there are those people, who I suspect make up a disproportionately large number of the remainder, who are painfully aware of the genuine gaps in their expertise and knowledge. Regardless of their curiosity, openness to learn and proven expertise, they appear inhibited and sometimes incapacitated by the looming spectre of what they do not know, or do not do, expertly.

In this chapter, I will discuss how to reframe your perceived gaps as unique opportunities or strengths to boost self-assurance and effectiveness. It is essential to see the opportunity for growth differently than it's been spun for you most of your life.

- Developmental gaps are not an inherent sign of a weak intellect.
- Developmental gaps are not an inherent personal or organisational brand risk.

- Talking about development gaps and desired growth doesn't make you weak; it is essential in making yourself available for evolution.

This chapter will not create a narrative where every weakness or deficit you have can be turned into a strength. Personal growth is not about turning everything into a hidden strength. It's about turning the light on – and not flinching at what you see and being willing to objectively consider what must be improved now, and what can wait. It's as much about improving our critical perception, decision-making and prioritisation as any particular deficit.

ACCURATE SELF-ASSESSMENT

Evolution is impossible if, when we look at ourselves, we treat our weaknesses like a job interview question – ignoring anything potentially real and informative, and instead offering some banal, rehearsed deflection: 'I care too much', or 'I can be a bit of a perfectionist'. The implication is always the same – that the flaw isn't real, and certainly isn't a liability. It's just a different flavour of excellence.

On the other hand, every day I meet someone who appears oblivious to the point of stretching incredulity when asked about their strengths. They name the most inane aspects of themselves and describe them in a way so devoid of context or meaning that they sound trivial.

Even high performers often undersell themselves out of habit or socialised modesty. I coached an exceptional business leader recently. In preparation for her interviews for a well-earned senior role, I asked about her great qualities, and she said, 'I'm hard-working'.

I could practically see her future interview panel's eyes roll in unison at that statement. I am not telling you that being hard-working isn't important, but a few probing questions later, and we are getting into qualities that underpin that broad label and transcend it. The descriptions of her character and qualities at a more granular level helped me, and I think helped her, to see how remarkable she is.

One of the first weaknesses we can address is the inability to see and accurately describe our strengths.

Here are some filters to use when considering your own approach to describing your skills.

Granularity

The more granularly we describe a positive trait or characteristic, the less likely it is to sound 'icky' when you say it in your head or out loud. We all know how insufferable that (usually successful) braggart in your office is. We recoil from that approach so much as to end up in a dimension where saying anything positive about ourselves feels dangerous. However, the more granular you can be with your description, the more you can grant people access to your skillset without experiencing the 'ick'.

My brain works interestingly, and I've been working on understanding it over the years. I notice this brain quirk especially when

I coach people, especially those from sectors or industries with which I am less familiar. I've learned that if I listen actively and intently, it's like Tetris is happening in my mind. (If some graduate students I teach read this, they may need to know this before I go on: Tetris is a game from the 1980s where different-shaped blocks fall, and you rotate them to fit together and clear rows.)

Even when I am listening to unfamiliar context, technical terms and acronyms, I can see the pieces of information of all different shapes falling and turning in my mind, all without my active intervention and eventually, if I remain unclenched, a last piece I've been waiting for will fall and *Brrrpp* (that's the noise the game makes when you eliminate four lines at once or 'get a Tetris'), I understand and can give a plausible response or ask a sensible question.

Ask yourself, when describing how my brain works, does that:

- Help others to imagine how they might 'use' me more effectively?
- Sound better than, 'I'm just naturally intelligent!'

I am sure my brain quirk involves biology, genetics and environmental components, but I choose how and if I use that function. Denying it on the basis 'it's not *all* me', or being more generic, only does me a disservice.

When acknowledging your strengths or accomplishments, be specific and detailed rather than making broad claims. Use anecdotes or your own, more personal understanding of the strength to describe it more effectively. This granular approach helps you communicate your value effectively without sounding boastful or triggering discomfort in yourself or others.

Externalisation

Sometimes called 'attributional externality', externalisation is the tendency to locate causes for what happens to us, to an outside source or force. In this context, it's when we attribute to circumstance, luck or someone else's largess the entirety of the reason we have a positive trait.

We all do it in one context or another, and it has roots in socialised expectations of humility ('I'm not brilliant at this; I just went to a good university') so that you don't 'make other people feel stupid', for example. Still, those rules don't seem to apply equally to everyone, and it appears to me that following those rules disproportionately advances some people over others. Forget that rule and own what you do well.

Accurately own your skills, competencies and intellect, even if you think you didn't 'earn' them or that they're genetic or otherworldly gifts. Attributing them elsewhere facilitates being overlooked and your skill less highly regarded, even if it's noticed.

Transferability

This is the idea that people recognise that having one set of competencies means a likelihood that they will also be competent or at least quick to learn in another domain. Even when people have a decent self-assessment and understand their skills, they often fall into the trap of thinking that weaknesses are always areas where they don't have skills, and they are not.

I can't ski. I never learned. I wasn't allowed to in my NBA contract back in the day, and now, with a fragile back and knees, I am not looking to speed down the slopes and prematurely end up in the hospital. My lack of chops on the slopes is not a weakness; in my context, it's an irrelevance. I'd imagine if I decided to switch careers and become a ski instructor or even live where skiing is how you get around, I'd be at a disadvantage, but context matters for weaknesses.

I mention this because often the areas we aren't experts in are adjacent or related to places where we have skill, and we can have significant faith in the fact that transference will occur, allowing us to be quick studies in this new area.

Somewhere in the recesses of my mind are muscle memories of summers spent roller skating and ice skating as well as skateboarding (well before it was cool!), and were my knees not now made of chalk, I fancy myself a skier, if only for the 'après' bit.

Recognise that skills are transferable across related domains, so don't label all skill gaps as weaknesses. Instead, have confidence that your existing competencies will help you learn quickly in adjacent areas when necessary. True weaknesses are only relevant when they matter in your specific context.

Learning Willingness Quotient (LWQ)

The learning willingness quotient (otherwise known as the learning quotient[1] or learnability) measures a person's motivation and openness to learning. It's a quality, not a deficit.

Having things to learn is a sign of being human and conscious. Omniscience is a mythical quality that people valorise and assign to the gods, but, like immortality, I can only imagine these traits as a source of devastating, everlasting mundanity.

Still, many of us get to a point where we fear sharing our willingness to learn as if it were a proxy for our inexpertise. Open curiosity, wonder and intrigue are signs of a healthy 'willingness quotient' and if people around you see that differently, that's often because many people in positions of power rely on maintaining their position by ensuring the stupefaction of those around them and the curious and willing to learn are a threat to their world order.

Embrace your willingness to learn as a strength, not a weakness. Don't hide your learning orientation out of fear that it suggests inexperience – those who discourage curiosity often do so to maintain their own power position rather than to support your development.

Contingent Self-Worth

When your sense of value depends entirely on specific achievements, skills or external validation, you create a precarious foundation for confidence. In professional settings, this manifests as people who swing between overconfidence when succeeding and complete devastation when facing setbacks – people whose sense of self vacillates at the whim of external factors. They may refuse opportunities outside their comfort zone, fearing failure would confirm their profound insecurities: watch for the colleague who cannot receive constructive feedback without personalising it as a total rejection.

When your worth is contingent on performance in narrow domains, you become trapped in proving yourself rather than growing yourself. Instead, recognise that your inherent value exists independently from any specific skill or accomplishment – this creates the psychological safety needed to take reasonable risks and embrace learning opportunities without existential dread.

It is true that after conscientious effort, a pattern may occur in domains where you are not best equipped, but even that conclusion is about a skill deficiency, not a personal dysfunction.

Practise outcome-neutral language by describing specific processes rather than making sweeping self-judgements. Say, 'My approach to this project was effective' rather than 'I'm brilliant', and say, 'That strategy didn't work this time' rather than 'I'm a failure!' This linguistic shift creates psychological distance between outcomes and your core identity, enabling more objective self-assessment and resilience.

Take it from a kid who spent years looking at random stuff under a microscope – everything looks gross (if interesting) when you look at it too closely (seriously, try it!) – so a bit of psychological distance helps us have a more practical perspective.

Sufficiency

Sufficiency refers to the honed sense that people have adequate capabilities to attempt and likely succeed at a task or role, even without mastery of all relevant skills. In part, this is because they acknowledge their ability to learn, extrapolate from skills they know they have, and recognise the nuanced picture that in any context, project or role, some skills are mandatory, while some are, if not irrelevant, certainly optional – at least to get started.

This is not about confidence but rather a nuanced and informed perspective on the task demand relative to the skills at hand.

A good example of some socialised differences in people's sense of sufficiency is the often-cited internal study conducted at Hewlett-Packard, which found that women typically applied for jobs only when they met 100% of the qualifications listed. In comparison, men applied when they met about 60% of the qualifications. In newer research, we know this isn't about women's 'confidence', but a more nuanced picture including perceptions of fairness in hiring processes, the environmental risks of asserting themselves as qualified and differential interpretations of job requirements.

Apply the 60% rule – if you possess about 60% of the required capabilities for a role or task, you likely have sufficient skills to succeed. Recognise that in stretch environments and during times of change and organisational transformation, no one has 100% of what's needed, and your ability to establish some of the core capabilities mentioned in this book and then adapt and learn beyond that is as valuable as your existing knowledge.

Value proposition clarity

Have confidence in articulating how one's unique combination of skills and attributes would benefit an organisation despite not matching the exact qualification profile. I believe that people have inherent value, but organisations tend to need proof. You'd think a track record of achievement would do the trick, but all too often, people need a narrative – a pithy 'elevator pitch' like the cover of this book, which is littered with phrases I hope to induce people to buy it, open it and see the value inside.

Creating this involves looking beyond the narrow confines of a job description to identify the underlying problems an organisation is trying to solve and positioning yourself as a distinctive solution.

Consider the case of a marketing executive who lacked apparently essential technical qualifications but secured a leadership role at a tech firm by demonstrating how her consumer psychology expertise could translate complex products into compelling customer narratives – something the technically qualified candidates couldn't offer. Or the lawyer who successfully moved into healthcare administration by showing how his litigation experience made him uniquely equipped to navigate regulatory compliance and risk management. They reframed their 'non-standard' backgrounds, some with 'obvious' technical gaps, as complementary perspectives rather than deficiencies in each case.

There is something distasteful in even telling you to create this stack of sentences that supposedly sum up your value, but know I am speaking about your value in a very narrow context to act as an accessibility aid – subtitles, to help those who look at you like they're watching a foreign film, to get with the plot.

Map your unique skills to your organisation's actual challenges rather than just the listed requirements of your job. Prepare at least three specific examples where your unusual combination of experiences solved problems in unexpected ways, and practise articulating them in under 90 seconds each. This 'distinctive value story' will differentiate you more effectively than attempting to prove how you match a standardised profile.

Self-Effacement

People from certain cultures, faiths and socioeconomic circumstances, as well as people with disabilities and people who aren't men (and men who don't conform to dominant masculine norms) are regularly socially programmed and therefore predisposed to be humble-to-a-fault.

At the end of this chapter, I will add the whole 'Humility Trap' definition from *The Promises of Giants*, so you can see it described in full, but for now, let me quote myself – hardly self-effacing, I know, to say:

> 'It is no less a lie to tell someone you lack skills, characteristics or qualities you possess than to claim to have a set of competencies that you do not'.

All the societies that socially programme some of their population to be demure and self-effacing also say they strongly oppose lying.

When it comes to self-effacement, dimming your light is not humility – it is a quiet betrayal of your effort, excellence, and future.

In this context, I say:

> Don't lie for the comfort of people who care about you less, for your effort to spare them your light.
>
> Don't lie to anyone about your contributions or capabilities that will otherwise be misappropriated.

Consider the brilliant software engineer who consistently attributes her coding breakthroughs to 'the team' despite working through weekends to solve problems others couldn't crack. Or the teacher who dismisses praise for transforming struggling students' performance as 'just doing my job' rather than acknowledging his exceptional pedagogical skills.

These aren't just random examples of modesty – they represent systemic patterns in which talented individuals from certain backgrounds diminish their contributions while others confidently claim credit for collective achievements.

This self-effacement becomes particularly problematic in competitive environments like job interviews, promotion discussions or funding applications, where articulating your value isn't optional but essential.

Many highly capable professionals are passed over not because they lack skills, but because they've been conditioned to believe that honesty about their excellence is arrogance.

Write a short 'credit statement' for one of your latest successes. One paragraph. No 'team', no qualifiers, no externalisation, no apologies. Just write what you did, what it achieved and why it mattered.

Then say it aloud until it feels true – because it is.

Help Them, Help You

One of the often overlooked team-based positives of individuals' capacity to describe their skills and competencies accurately is the ability to assist colleagues in knowing what skills are available to solve emerging organisational problems.

Even great leaders are drawn to blatant self-interest, and if you can describe your skills in a way that helps them, it will help you too.

I keep hearing there is a war for talent (war and sports metaphors in business are galling to me, in part because they are so often used by leaders who operate with a recklessness that no elite military force would countenance and a skill level that no professional team would tolerate, but I digress). Despite this supposed paucity of talent in the market, my team and I go into businesses every day and hidden in plain sight is talent that has been missed, usually through a combination of organisational myopia and individuals who can't describe their potential and skills in a way others can recognise. In one financial institution we worked with, we found one man who went through our STARs™ programme – where robust coaching and group sessions build skills in self-assessment and description of competencies (and some work with myopic hiring managers!) – and immediately went for a new role and got it, after six previous failed attempts at that level.

Another programme participant had been in her role for 16 years. Sixteen years!

Six months after participating in STARs™, she was in a new, more senior role that she and several other senior leaders, including her new manager, acknowledged she'd been capable of for over a decade.

If you think staying quiet about your strengths is generous or modest, it's neither. It's organisational self-sabotage. You're invisible talent, which hurts your team as much as your chances.

List three specific skills you have that your team or organisation underuses. Then, write one or two sentences for each to clarify how that skill helps solve a real business problem. Share it in your next one-to-one or team meeting. Don't wait to be discovered. Be findable.

You can use these same filters when considering your weaknesses or areas for development, too. No doubt you considered some flaws even as you read the previous section about strengths, so I'll summarise some thoughts and takeaways specific to flaws here:

- *Granularity:* Vague labels like 'bad communicator' or 'not strategic enough' often provoke shame or denial. Describing a flaw or area for development with granular detail helps make it specific and solvable. Being precise reduces emotional weight and allows others to offer targeted support or feedback. Choose one weakness and describe it in one sentence using clear, specific terms. Then add a second sentence on what you're doing to improve. Clarity reduces shame and increases support.

- *Externalisation:* When we blame external forces – circumstance, luck, background – for our weaknesses, we remove ourselves from the equation. While context always matters, and it is undoubtedly true that sometimes forces beyond our control conspire against us, abdicating responsibility entirely robs us of agency and growth. If you're blaming something external for a weakness, reframe it: 'Yes, this was shaped by X, but here's what I contributed to this problem and what I can do about it now'.

- *Transferability:* Not knowing how to do something is not the same as being incapable. Many people confuse a lack of exposure with a fundamental flaw. Instead, recognise when a skill gap is in an adjacent area where other strengths can apply. Look at a weakness and ask: 'What do I already know that could help me build this skill faster than someone starting from scratch?'

- *Learning Willingness Quotient (LWQ):* Some people mistake having something to learn as a weakness, rather than a strength of mindset. LWQ is about how open you are to growth, and it's often more predictive of success than existing competence. Write down one area you want to grow in. Then write why it matters to you and how you demonstrate (or will demonstrate) a willingness to improve. Share this with someone you trust with a deadline for checking back in, to create accountability.

- *Contingent Self-Worth:* Every flaw feels catastrophic when your value is tied to success or failure in one area. This stifles experimentation, learning and growth. Decoupling identity from performance enables resilience. Reframe your internal narrative. Instead of 'I failed', say 'This didn't work – what can I learn from this? What actions must I take to ensure success the next time?' Track how this language shift affects your willingness to try again.

- *Sufficiency:* Many overestimate what's required to try something new and underestimate their own readiness. A flaw doesn't have to be fixed entirely before you begin. Sometimes 'good enough to start' is more than enough. For any task you're hesitating on, ask: 'If someone else in the team I trusted, with similar skills to my own, tried this, would I think they were ready?' If yes, proceed as if you are. Or ask, 'Would (and indeed did) my trusted team member or boss trust me with this task? What must that mean about me having enough to complete it?'

- *Value Proposition Clarity:* Weaknesses feel bigger when you can't clearly explain your strengths. Knowing and articulating what you offer makes your gaps feel smaller and more manageable. Write three sentences that connect your current strengths to a real need in your organisation. This anchors your development areas in a broader, more strategic frame.

- *Self-Effacement:* Dismissing or hiding your strengths can lead others to overemphasise your weaknesses. In competitive environments, silence is often misread as absence. Overcorrecting for humility hides your true capabilities. Choose one success and write a credit statement that names exactly what you did, without qualifiers. Say it aloud until you can say it without hesitation or apology.

- *Help Them, Help You:* If others don't know your skills, they can't help you grow them. Being explicit about your work challenges or areas where you feel less well-equipped allows others to offer relevant opportunities, feedback or resources. Tell your manager or a peer one area you're actively developing and one way they could support or stretch you. Invite them into your growth, not just the results.

There is little in this world that comes without some discomfort, and evolution here, reframing and ameliorating relevant weaknesses, will feel a little uncomfortable.

One way I reframe my gaps is to expose myself to things I know nothing about on purpose! It is thrilling! I dive into something I know nothing about but am interested in, and see what happens. From *kintsugi* (the Japanese art of mending the broken pieces of ceramics using lacquer mixed with powdered gold, silver or platinum) to the previously mentioned 'phatic expressions', there is a wealth of insight out there you'll be as clueless about as I am, and at least potentially, as enriched by learning about them. It helps me, I think, to see the 'stuff I don't know' as 'stuff I haven't yet invested in yet', rather than some inherent weakness. At first, it felt important that there was some subject-matter distance from my own area of expertise – hence the *kintsugi,* which helped me to see the absence of knowledge or expertise differently, and that exposure now helps me create an appropriate psychological distance in areas of intellectual debt adjacent to or within the scope of my expertise.

To evolve, we must learn to collaborate with ourselves. Shame and silence don't make strong foundations. To help you evolve, I want to introduce one more thing – a process called motivational interviewing (MI). MI is a counselling methodology developed by William R. Miller and Stephen Rollnick in the 1980s to support individuals struggling with ambivalence about change.

I first thought about including this concept in this book when the temporary TikTok phenomenon of 'We listen but we don't judge' was everywhere online – a trend where people, often colleagues or partners, would say something they had been doing that the other didn't know about and likely would disapprove.

MI has a series of principles, a little more involved than simply 'listening without judgement', but a practical, evidence-based framework for confronting both our own evolution – facing strengths and challenges alike – and how we support others through theirs. Here is a practical summary of these principles:

- *Express Empathy* (the 'listen, but don't judge' part!): Demonstrate a deep, non-judgemental understanding of another person's internal experience. Reflective listening (reframing the points and emotions you witness) shows that the person's feelings, fears, and hesitations are seen.

- *Develop Discrepancy:* Being a humanistic psychologist at heart, I love this part. I help individuals explore the incongruence – the gap between where they are and where they want to be. This tension can create substantial motivation for change.

- *Roll with Resistance:* Instead of confronting resistance head-on, explore it. Anytime you begin to examine weaknesses and for many people when they begin to be granular about strengths, there will be resistence. Instead of forcing change, citing your experience or wisdom, work to understand the reluctance as part of the process.

- *Support Self-Efficacy:* Build the person's belief in their ability to change. Being stuck in any status quo can allow people to conflate familiarity with happiness, so even the most minor changes can feel difficult and unwelcome. Celebrating any and all small wins, especially early on in the change phase, is essential, and re-emphasising where you've had past successes can fuel confidence.

- *Evoke Change Talk:* Encourage individuals to discover and articulate their reasons and desires for change. Changing for someone else is not always futile, but it's harder and less sustainable than changing for a reason centred on and around the individual. Motivation is far more effective when spoken from the self, not imposed externally, even when that's done out of love.
- *Collaborate with Yourself:* Be an active, compassionate participant in your own growth. Don't bully yourself or others into change, whether with discursively violent inner monologue or

---

Principles into Practice: Making it Real
The Credit Statement Challenge

Write a one-paragraph account of a recent success. No 'we', no 'just', no humility qualifiers. Start with: *'I contributed. . .'* and describe what you did, what it achieved, and why it mattered.

   Say it aloud until it feels natural – because it's true.

One Flaw, Two Sentences

Pick a weakness. Describe it in one clear, neutral sentence. Then write a second sentence outlining what you are doing to improve it.

   Clarity is more useful than shame.

Ask for a Mirror

Choose a peer or mentor and ask: *'What's one strength you've witnessed in me that I don't mention enough?'*

Record (with permission) or take detailed notes on what they say.

Then reflect on what's stopping you from naming it yourself.

Keep the recording/transcript as a reminder and revisit occasionally to see if your embrace of the quality has changed.

Transfer Confidence Audit

Choose a task or role you're hesitant about. Write down three existing skills or experiences that could transfer to help you succeed.

Confidence isn't just personality – it's evidence.

Curiosity Investment

Spend 20 minutes this week exploring something unrelated to your role – an art, science or idea you know nothing about. Chapters 9 and 3 provide many examples of how to find these topics.

Notice what it teaches you about the joy and discomfort of being a beginner.

Self-Worth Language Shift

Replace 'I am good/bad at X' with 'My last attempt at X went well/poorly because. . .'. Describe the action or plan that failed and your part in that, but don't automatically conflate what you did, or the success or otherwise of an outcome, with who you are.

(Continued)

Listen to yourself and others around you for language that conflates missteps and mistakes with fundamental moral, psychological or intellectual flaws.

Language shapes mindset. Track how this reframing changes your internal dialogue.

Motivational Interviewing Summary Table for Quick Reference

MI Principle	Leadership Application
Express Empathy	Show people you *see* them before you try to guide or develop them
Develop Discrepancy	Highlight how actions align or conflict with personal goals or team identity
Roll with Resistance	Use resistance as a lens into values, concerns or unmet needs – not a threat.
Support Self-Efficacy	Reflect people's strengths back to them and connect to past success.
Evoke Change Talk	Ask open questions that invite individuals to narrate their case for change.
Collaborate with Yourself	Shift internal dialogue from blame to curiosity; model growth-in-progress rather than 'instant perfection'.

an external approach. To me, this principle is especially powerful for leaders navigating self-doubt, burnout, or stretching for growth at the edges of their expertise – or indeed, for those leaders supporting team members doing the same.

THE HUMILITY TRAP

The humility trap is the tendency of some people to under-emphasise, caveat or diminish their positive qualities in self-reflection and conversation with others. This occurs to avoid any chance that their description will be misinterpreted as arrogance or bravado, no matter how inconceivable.

Additionally, it encourages the disproportionate emphasis and continual re-examination of even minor flaws or areas for development. These aspects of the humility trap create a damaged image of a person's capability and potential.

Whether in conversation during networking activities, personal or professional development planning sessions, when volunteering for new or stretch projects at work or speaking to an interview panel for a new role, the humility trap is a devastating impediment to success.

The humility trap impacts more than just face-to-face interactions. The allergy to appearing remotely conceited or self-important is so overwhelming that it can prevent people from concisely and accurately articulating their strengths, even to themselves. As such, even in situations that demand a person to explain their skills, the quality and clarity of any description can be so generic and equivocal as to give the distinct impression that the skills may not exist at all.

The malignant blindspot this phenomenon creates can fundamentally misalign a person's individual sense of agency, accomplishment and potential. This prevents the fair and objective analysis of their positive traits. Since no such impediment for proportional scrutiny of areas for development exists within the humility trap, this will usually lead to developing an overly critical and negative self-image.

The humility trap does not impact all people equally. Some educational and socio-economic pathways literally teach a form of 'professional self-promotion', and there are distinct differences across gender, culture, ethnicity, religion and geography, not to mention the relative familiarity and similarity of a person to their environment that dictate the impact the humility trap will have on them.

When it comes to the humility trap, spot it, name it, and refuse to be ruled by it.

CHAPTER EIGHT

NAVIGATING NOVEL AND FRACTIOUS ENVIRONMENTS

IT'S NOT MAGIC. . . IT'S ADAPTABILITY

Every day, I check my various feeds and resources to stay informed while doing my best not to become jaded by it all. A handful of people in this world might be so wealthy or otherwise powerful as to be functionally immune from the tempestuous, antagonistic, febrile and unpredictable world the rest of us live in. I take some solace in knowing enough about most of these very public characters to know they aren't reading this book. But for you and me, we must navigate novel and fractious environments daily.

Novel and fractious environments aren't only the result of global unrest or dramatic headlines. They take shape in the quiet tension between colleagues who don't trust one another, in meetings where nobody speaks candidly, and in cultures where outcomes trump principles. They're present in the split-second decision to challenge a senior leader's rhetoric or to stay silent. They show up when values collide with targets, when loyalty is weaponised, and when people with power interpret dissent as betrayal. Sometimes they erupt in obvious ways, like the shock announcement of yet another business 'transformation'; more often, they fester in withheld feedback, silent complicity, and the quiet erosion of psychological safety. Adaptability in these settings isn't tactical – it's existential.

I want to start with a disclaimer.

There was a time when I gave embarrassingly privileged advice. I wish I could say this was during grad school – the naïveté of youth – but it was more like a decade ago. I would recommend actions that were, frankly, inaccessible to many people. Things like 'get therapy', as if that were freely available, affordable or culturally safe. Or I'd suggest strategies that – with all the best will in the world – could have put someone at risk in front of an unreasonable employer.

Let me be clear: I want no economic martyrs on my hands.

So I need you to view this chapter through the lens of the privileges you enjoy – or the lack of them you endure. I'm not suggesting you shy away from discomfort or become unwilling to act. It's just that, in this world, where the social safety net is more theory than reality, you must weigh my advice against your own context and the needs of those who rely on you most.

Your safety matters more to me than your adherence to my recommendations.

Read this with boldness, yes – but read with care.

UNDERSTANDING FRACTIOUS ENVIRONMENTS

Fractiousness isn't always loud. It lives in quiet dysfunctions – the unspoken tensions, the ethical compromises made to meet deadlines, and the leaders who value loyalty over truth and the perpetuation of their own power over the dignity of others. Environments like these require a different kind of intelligence – not simply IQ, but adaptive acuity: the ability to sense, shift and stay philosophically, psychologically and ethically intact when the context is anything but.

Sometimes, no malice is intended or implied, and an environment can still be fractious.

When I first moved to America to attend high school, I was a stranger in a strange land. I arrived in August at Toledo's regional airport, and when the plane door opened, I experienced a wave of heat I'd never imagined possible on earth.

I walked towards the arrival gates on the tarmac and to baggage claim. As I entered the space, I quickly realised that all the sweat I had gathered from the two-minute walk outside was now freezing on my body due to the air-conditioning that only I seemed to notice was overzealous. After a warm handshake with my high school coach for the next 12 months, we waited for my world to arrive in two suitcases, and he began what I imagine was an epic pep talk designed to make me feel welcome and motivate me for the year ahead. He might as well have been speaking Martian, and to begin, I let it wash over me, slightly panicking with that feeling we've all had when introduced to a new environment: 'Will it always be like this?', 'I'll never understand a word that anyone says!' and more. Then I realised that I could get the gist of what was being conveyed if I had a total focus and tried to absorb every element of context available. The wave of a hand, the slight scrunch of an eye, and the more obvious pointing at things as we walked to his car.

It appeared to me that he somehow understood most of what I said back, and his face never showed an expression that told me I was way off. However, it is confusing on reflection that we assumed the other would be familiar, similar and unfazed by each other and in my case, my surroundings.

I think it's the kind of assumption that only happens when you've rarely, if ever, travelled outside of your 'home' bubble, something that can happen regardless of whether you have a passport or not. I had a passport, and it was certainly true for me – after all, my only knowledge of America before being there was the TV shows I watched before bed – *Knight Rider* and the *A-Team* – and I understood them just fine! It took a while to realise *Knight Rider*, with its sweeping Pacific backgrounds, was not set in Ohio.

When I spoke to Coach around other players, their reactions and comments provided additional context that allowed me to understand what was expected of me. A few of them, whom I noticed had realised I sometimes got lost when new people talked to me and whom I had subsequently approached to help me understand, would silently nudge and cajole me to ensure I complied even before the meaning of an instruction sank in.

I was a few exhausting days into living in Toledo before understanding that I must create time to acclimatise and give myself a chance to adapt properly. I also understood that my approach would get me there, but would mean compromises and fatigue. I was tired all the time, already an introvert in the country where there seemed so few, I was interpersonally exhausted by the overt expressions of welcome, and I was already softening the 't' in water to a 'd', to avoid the monotonous ridicule as much as communicate effectively.

I knew the 'fake it until you make it' approach, which is always less of a strategy than simply 'hoping nobody notices!' wouldn't work. Instead, this strategy for surviving novel environments where friction might come from misunderstanding required more calculation and personal evolution.

In unfamiliar, fractious spaces, clarity often hides in subtext.

Adaptability begins with a particular kind of perceptive listening where you switch from a sole focus on the inpenetrable code you're experiencing, whether that's words or unfamiliar processes. Instead, you widen your view to encompass every other conceivable data point outside of the ones that are confounding you, to draw context and understand the confusing and potentially contentious by looking at what it isn't.

As you may already know, you can't consistently – and in workplaces I want to say, often – rely on your environment to recognise the need for leeway, patience and a more tailored approach to support your induction. In the business world now, one of the sexiest phrases bandied about by recruiters and hiring managers is, 'Can they hit the ground running?'

I always think that concept is a clear misunderstanding of sustainable high performance, given that it doesn't differentiate between someone with the skills, willingness and capacity to easily adapt to any new change and people who have no ability, but because of their past role doesn't require any adaptation for the role as it stands. Being quick to 'fit in' and understand all the acronyms seems like a really sensible criteria but it's no indicator of a person's potential, and might actually be a sign they are less interested in stretching and growth – something I think we can all agree is a key characteristic in this world of change.

Adapting to fractious environments means understanding the environment and communication by:

- Resisting focusing only on what you don't understand
- Use every available surrounding context to make sense of what you don't know – there are clues everywhere
- Give yourself a grace period: 'hitting the ground running' is less important than quickly becoming the fastest runner

- Don't expect everyone to see what you don't understand; be prepared to be vulnerable with a select few people
- Recruit relationships with translators who can clue you in on the key information and norms
- Commit to induction, but not assimilation – you don't have to lose everything you are to belong – and if you do, we'd normally call that environment a cult
- Existing in a novel and/or fractious environment is exhausting; find ways to 'fill your cup'.

THE COST OF BROADENING SOMEONE'S NARROW FOCUS

One of the main benefits leaders cite when bringing new people to their environment is the ability to 'see what others are no longer able to'. They often fail to mention that many, and perhaps most, people already in that environment, which is so new to you, don't always revel in the observations of an outsider.

In fact, your 'new' observations can often generate friction.

These bosses seeking new insights from those previously on the outside are right: their organisations have grown oblivious to much of what happens within their walls. When a group becomes hyper-fixated on a single task, goal, belief or source of validation, it becomes insensitive to what's unfolding around it – unable to register nuance, tension, quiet dissent or spot internal opportunities and talent.

Indeed, some organisations fail to see just how unusual their operation has become, perhaps to the point of limiting who might want to work there and how normalised some quite strange behaviours are.

I have done videos on LinkedIn reacting to a CEO prowling around a stage proudly proclaiming, 'You can't work here unless you have a six pack'. And I honestly don't think he thinks what a strange (never mind discriminatory) statement that is!

I still remember being invited to my first American wrestling match. As a Brit raised on the theatrics of 'Big Daddy' versus 'Giant Haystacks', British wrestlers in the WWE mould, so I expected pantomime. Instead, I saw wiry teens twisting over each other in skintight singlets – and then one moment, when two wrestlers stood up, it was clear that the friction had become too much! I looked around to see who else had noticed. No one. Not a single flicker of discomfort from a crowd I had already begun to notice had 'politico-moral' approaches to 'decency' quite different from mine. Even from the kids at the centre of this match, they just played on.

I'm not trying to titillate or shame in this example, but it does show how context can create desensitisation. In this space, these boys could wear something as revealing as a wrestling singlet, but that freedom appeared very contained to me, never mind anything else that was going on. I am certain that asking about the conventions around wrestling and what I witnessed would have been controversial and costly, so I kept it to myself.

I recognise this is not some earth-shattering revelation, but the same rules apply when you enter novel and fractious environments of all kinds. These environments will have developed 'inattentional blindness', where people fail to notice an otherwise unexpected object or event in plain sight because their attention is focused elsewhere.

The *Invisible Gorilla*[1] experiment showed how inattentional blindness prevents people from seeing even obvious anomalies when focused on something else, no matter the importance or complexity of that something else. In this research, half the people watching a basketball game were told to count the number of passes for one team, and they completely missed that a man in a gorilla suit walked into the shot for nine seconds!

In any novel environment, you can be seen as the cause of fractiousness by speaking out and saying what you see plainly that others have become inured to. Equally, when entering an environment that is already fractious, just asking the questions and making the observations that might otherwise be considered 'doing your job' can be a form of self-harm. As such, here are some guiding ideas to reduce the risk of harm to you, your career or your reputation from saying what you see.

I am fully aware that any culture that brings people in on the basis of wanting to hear new voices and authentic perspectives shouldn't require this, but we live in the real world here:

- *Choose your moment with intent.* Psychological safety fluctuates situationally.[2] Research shows that speaking up is better received when the timing aligns with a recognised need. Don't just look for your moment – look for an individual or organisational appetite for your insight or opportunity created by external pressures.

- *Frame your insight as a contribution, not a critique.* Use 'I've noticed something I think could help. . .' instead of 'This isn't working'. Framing differentiates between being seen as disruptive and being seen as valuable.[3]

- *Invite others in before they feel implicated.* Pre-empt defensiveness by expressing curiosity: 'Can you help me understand if I am missing something. . .'. This softens perceived confrontation and increases engagement without diluting your point.

- *Ground observations in shared goals or values.* Link your point to a team or organisational priority: 'Because we all care about X, I think this might be worth exploring. . .' suggests that anchoring your insight to a collective purpose reduces the perceived threat.

- *Use specific, observable language.* Avoid abstract or accusatory phrasing. Focus on behaviours and outcomes, not personalities or motives: 'In the last three meetings, we haven't discussed Y', rather than 'You always ignore Y'.

- *Test the waters in lower-stakes spaces.* Trial your observation in a one-to-one with a trusted peer or ally first. Individual feedback can help refine delivery and gauge political risk before wider exposure.[4]

- *Signal alliance, not insurrection.* Use language that signals inclusion and forward momentum: 'We could strengthen this by. . .' or 'What would it take for us to. . .?' This reduces the instinctive pushback triggered by perceived disruption.
- *Know your exit and escalation paths.* If sharing what you know goes poorly, protect your psychological and professional well-being by knowing when to step back, escalate or document. For the latter, documentation, when sharing insights that challenge the status quo in work settings, I recommend ensuring that everything is always documented. Courage doesn't require career martyrdom.

'DO YOU WANT TO WIN OR BE RIGHT?'

I first introduced this concept in *The Promises of Giants*. This question challenges our egos. In full, I'd say, 'Do you want to be right, right now, or do you want to win in the long term?'

This decision doesn't always mean biting your tongue, placating others or presenting a poker face, although I tend to find those features common. Sometimes, it simply isn't the right moment. The people in the room may have no appetite to hear from you, and acting now wouldn't get you what you actually want.

This isn't about missing a quick win; it's about choosing between a strategic, temporary side- or back-step and a pyrrhic victory.

In novel environments, being 'right, right now' can feel like you're immediately 'adding value', so the temptation is to exhume every organisational misstep, every gap in logic or process – and in doing so, find yourself unpopular.

Being 'right, right now' might feel (or even *be*) righteous in fractious environments, but it doesn't always serve the greater good – or your own.

Managing your voice in novel or fractious contexts means tuning into the organisation's 'implicit voice' rules – those unwritten, often unspoken beliefs that guide when people speak up and when to remain silent.

These rules don't always originate with a toxic boss. Sometimes, they're inherited – shaped by home, school, community or past workplaces. You carry them with you, too. So before you speak, it's worth asking: What are the 'implicit voice' rules I'm following, and who wrote them?

Strategic restraint isn't weakness.

Choosing your battles based on a long-term, purpose-led plan, rather than a short-term grudge, is a mark of maturity. Sometimes, letting others feel they've won is exactly what you do when playing the long game.

There are a few things to consider when deciding whether to be 'right, right now' or win in the longer term.

Decision Aid: Speak Now or (Temporarily) Hold Your Peace?

Before you decide to speak up, ask yourself:

1. What is the real goal here?

   Do I want to:

   A. Silence a critic

   B. Solve a problem

   C. Be seen

   D. Influence a direction

   E. Protect something important?

   If the answer is A or C, proceed at your own risk, or more sensibly, don't. If there is an enjoyable rush as a work enemy is publicly vanquished or a mic-drop moment that select work fans congratulate you on afterwards, you likely picked 'right, right now'.

2. Will this land in fertile soil?

   Are the people in the room open, defensive, or distracted?

   Speaking truth in hostile conditions may satisfy your conscience, but not your purpose. Timing isn't everything – but it's a lot.

3. What am I risking, and what am I preserving?

   What's the reputational, relational or emotional cost of speaking now?

   What credibility *or trust might I preserve by waiting?*

Be honest: some moments (especially public moments) burn goodwill faster than they build clarity.

4. Is there a more strategic moment ahead?

   Will I have another opportunity to raise this when the stakes are clearer, the audience is more receptive, or my framing is more effective?

   Delaying isn't always avoidance – it's sometimes how influence works.

5. Am I prepared for the consequences?

   If my point is ignored, resisted or used against me, will I still be able to function in this space tomorrow with the same impact?

   If the answer is no, you may be choosing 'right, right now' over 'winning'.

6. What part of this is ego?

   Do I want to speak because I'm genuinely concerned, or because I want to prove a point?

   There's no shame in wanting credit. But clarity matters more than righteousness in the long term.

7. Whose voice am I following?

   Is my impulse to speak shaped by a past manager, cultural norm or family value that no longer fits?

   Before you act, check whose expectations you're living up to. This doesn't mean you should not speak, but be aware that incongruences in expectations of speaking up impact the effectiveness of the messages you send, regardless of how well your intervention is executed.

STRATEGIES FOR THRIVING IN CHALLENGING, DIVERSE OR ETHICALLY GREY CONTEXTS

Not every context rewards honesty, not every leader is fair, and not every team dynamic is salvageable. Thriving in fractious environments means adapting how you engage without compromising who you are. It requires quiet strength, not louder performance – a combination of ethical clarity, timing, and tactical patience.

Observe First, Speak Second

In complex dynamics, you learn more by noticing what's unsaid than by charging in. In unfamiliar or tense environments, your first job is to read the room, not rush to reframe it.

There is data everywhere: who interrupts, who gets deferred to, who rolls their eyes when someone speaks, who never speaks at all, and which combinations of people only communicate with each other. The unsaid – who gets credit, who absorbs blame, what jokes get told – often reveals more about the power structure than the stated values on the wall.

It's how you notice what others have grown desensitised to. You watch long enough to distinguish what is tolerated, feared and just below the surface.

This is not silence born of fear. This is observation as strategy. You aren't 'falling in' with whatever dysfunctions or hidden norms you see; you simply aren't crossing this new territory aimlessly until you understand where every trip wire or resource is.

Delay your intervention until your insights are grounded in patterns, not just moments.

Set Micro-Boundaries: Protecting Your Values in a Broken System

In systems where large-scale change feels out of reach – and in many workplaces, it does – your power often lies in what you do not allow to touch or distort you.

Micro-boundaries aren't about grand refusals or public declarations. They are the small, deliberate acts of principle that protect your integrity in toxic or ethically grey spaces. It's choosing not to laugh along when someone is undermined. It's correcting credit misattribution subtly but clearly. It's pronouncing someone's name correctly, even when others do not. It's staying out of whisper networks designed to harm rather than inform.

This isn't perfectionism – it's self-preservation. And over time, it sends a signal. Others notice that you remain upright in environments where others bend.

Micro-boundaries are also a way to preserve energy. You can't fight every fire, but you can stop the flames from breaching your sense of self.

List three behaviours, assumptions, or practices in your current environment you do not want to replicate or absorb. Decide how you will silently but consistently opt out.

Speak Strategically

Avoiding reckless candour when saying nothing isn't the answer. Adaptability means understanding what needs to be said, and when, how, and to whom.

In ethically complex or politically sensitive settings, being truthful isn't about volume but precision. You don't always need to speak first to be impactful (and like many other people in this space, I advise the more powerful people in any setting to speak last). You don't always need to say everything you know to demonstrate how clearly you see.

You might need to seed your idea in one meeting and fully land it in another. You might need to choose one person as a sponsor for the message rather than being its sole carrier.

Sometimes, speaking strategically means choosing language that protects your message long enough for it to take root.

I have played with the following phrase for some time and considered its addition to the book. I think this still holds true in most workplaces, at least in the UK and Europe, but I am no longer certain outside of those parameters:

> 'Being ignored loudly often does more harm than being heard quietly but effectively.'

This is true for people without all the necessary influence in a meeting room or 1-2-1 at work, but when I consider broader society, I am not sure that being 'quietly heard' is proving quite as effective as we all might have hoped.

Nonetheless, one skill we can all choose to learn is to distinguish between a *wise adaptation* in service of a greater good (for you and your organisation) and a *quiet betrayal* in service of the avoidance or reduction of personal discomfort in the moment. Both approaches are taxing, but in different ways:

- *Wise adaptation* is thoughtful, strategic and rarely spontaneous. It's an energy-expensive decision taken considering the consequences, and that cost is a calculated investment in something larger and more important than any individual moment.
- *Quiet betrayal* is the opposite. Although a decision may have loomed in your head for hours or days, it is far from strategic. As for cost, these decisions are taken to relieve tension, friction or discomfort in the moment, with no care for future consequences. This approach usually employs narrative revisionism in the immediate aftermath to ensure the choice feels inevitable on reflection.

A consistent characteristic difference between wise adaptation and quiet betrayal is their relative response to the passage of time. Wise adaptation decisions mature to become emblematic of who you say you are. In contrast, quiet betrayal beeps in your mind, like a smoke detector needing a battery change, even though it falls silent when you enter the room. It reminds us of something we should have done long ago as well as a reminder that we are less well protected for the decision.

Before speaking up, ask: 'Is this the right moment, with the right person, for the right (most strategic and meaningful) outcome?' If the answer is no, pause and plan for when it will be.

REFRAMING ADAPTABILITY AS AN ACT OF INTEGRITY

We've all experienced people who are whoever they need to be to get what they want. I think this is less adaptable than it is unmoored and opportunistic. Too often, adaptability is dismissed as 'chameleon' behaviour – code for compliance or slipperiness. But that's not what we mean here

True adaptability is principled fluidity – the capacity to shift your approach without surrendering your values. It is not about being whoever the room requires, but about knowing yourself well enough to adjust your method without distorting your meaning. It requires a deep understanding of your own core – what is essential, what must remain intact and what can flex to meet the moment without compromising who you are.

Adaptability is often mistaken for passivity, or worse, inconstancy. But at its best, adaptability is a discipline of integrity – the ability to move with the moment while anchoring to what matters most. It is how principled people survive – and influence – environments that might otherwise unmake them.

Adaptability isn't about being endlessly changeable – it's about staying coherent in a changing world.

Identify one non-negotiable value that anchors you, and one behaviour you're willing to flex in service of that value. Adapt around your core, not away from it.

YOUR CONTEXT, YOUR CALCULUS

One last reminder, which might well be a note for every chapter in this book: You are the only one who knows the risks you carry – economically, socially and psychologically. My role is not to demand bravery but to equip you with options.

I've seen people penalised in supposedly progressive workplaces while others are promoted for saying nothing. I've seen the same at immigration kiosks, in local shops and on the street when interacting with the police – all for speaking obvious truths.

That's why I no longer say 'be brave' without also saying 'be safe'.

Principles into Practice: Making it Real
The Flex Map

Draw two columns: 'Where I flex' and 'Where I hold'. List examples of recent decisions or dilemmas. Reflect on what these patterns reveal about how you adapt – and where you might over- or under-correct.

The Gorilla Check (based on the video where many watching didn't see the gorilla!)

Once a week, ask yourself: 'What am I not seeing because I'm focused on the wrong thing?'

Invite one trusted peer, friend or family member to answer for you from their perspective.

Pick a team member; really inhabit their life, relative experience and power. Look at the challenges your team is tasked with from their perspective. What else do you now see?

Adaptive Language Audit

Recall a meeting where you felt pressure to pretend to concur, agree to disagree, or conform to a group consensus. Replay it and ask:

- Where did I feel myself shift in tone or language?
- Was that a wise adaptation or a quiet betrayal of myself?

(Continued)

Pre-Mortem for Risky Conversations

Before a high-stakes conversation, write out the worst-case, best-case and most likely outcomes.

Ask yourself: 'What version of me does each require?'

Consider the likely ploys and phrases, whether designed or not, that are likely to trigger emotions or other responses.

Pre-plan your play. Never knowingly walk into a challenging conversation without this pre-mortem in place.

Adaptability means being ready for all three.

The 'Right vs Win' Journal

First write down a description of what 'winning' in the longer term really means to you in your context. The more vivid detail, the better a 'north star' that can be when considering decisions that take you towards that ('win in the longer term') versus take you in a different direction ('right, right now').

Then reflect on the past week, tease out the moments where you chose to be right, right now, versus win in the context you've illustrated.

For next week, track moments where you choose to be right and any you choose to be wrong. Reflect on what it cost you and what you gained from it.

Remember that often, even when it was the right decision strategically, it will have a personal or human cost for you that is worth considering over time.

PART III

AMPLIFYING IMPACT

CHAPTER NINE

LEARNING TO BUILD CONTEXTUAL INTELLIGENCE

IT'S NOT MAGIC. . . IT'S DELIBERATE REFLECTIVE PRACTICE

was talking with a friend and colleague recently, and he was talking in a genuinely generous way about how he loved to *know* things. He is truly learned and considered a boffin (technical term!) in his area of academia.

I considered replying in agreement, because I *do* love to know things, but another thought steamrolled it.

'What I *really* love is to learn things'.

It increasingly feels to me that everything I observe I can learn from (at least on reflection), and everything new I learn feels more like the 'penny drop' or 'Tetris' moments I described previously in Chapter 7.

Knowing things is valuable. But in leadership – and life – the real power lies in knowing which things matter most, in which moments, and why. Contextual intelligence is the ability to read the landscape around you, to join the dots between what you know and what is unfolding, and to adapt thoughtfully. It is a skill that grows not by chance, but by conscious reflection. This chapter is about building it – deliberately, practically and in ways that fit our real lives.

I feel much older than I did even five years ago, and my body reminds me of that fact every day, but my mind seems to respond to new insights and ideas like a child catching sight of an unfamiliar climbing frame: Their eyes light up as they see and barrel towards it, excited by the possibilities – somehow more enthused by the chance to test how their bodies can move within this new geometry, as by the bars themselves.

I am smiling as I write this, as I think of just some of the elements of learning that have improved my understanding to help me clarify and crystallise my thinking before sharing it with you. I often tell people that, for me, writing books is not a labour of love, but the learning it offers is most welcome.

That is the mindset shift required to augment our approach to this ever-changing world, moving from new learning as if a school kid: forced into it by 'overbearing' parents (or managers!) while looking plaintively out of the window, counting the minutes until 'play time' to a more receptive and reflective mode that builds contextual intelligence.

You, like me, may have hated (high) school, but there is an opportunity open to all of us to reconsider learning and reflection beyond crusty textbooks and inanimate subjects. And, instead, undertake a process of integrative reflection where new information is sought out and combined with other internal memories and experiences, as well as contextual information to form a more cohesive understanding of yourself, a more informed understanding of personal motives and a more well-rounded general perspective on your work and expertise.

To paraphrase MIT professor and author Donald Schön from his seminal book *The Reflective Practitioner: How Professionals Think in Action*,[1] integrative reflection enables learners to synthesise new learnings and experiences with prior knowledge to deepen understanding and accelerate professional growth.

In the context of this chapter, *integrative reflection* means:

- Revisiting diverse experiences (successes, failures, feedback, emotional responses, relationships, intentional and incidental learning opportunities)

- Synthesising learning across time and context rather than focusing on a single moment (considering what any new or reflected experience means in connection with others in your library of experiences, not just in isolation)
- Weighing the credibility or emotional weight of past experiences (considering the relative influence or importance of lessons, experiences or outcomes and indeed considering that you can't know the full scope of significance in isolation)
- Extracting actionable insight to guide future decisions, reactions or leadership choices (proactively connecting new learning and old to create wisdom and understanding, not just knowledge and data).

There doesn't seem to be one standard approach to integrative reflection, but I will list five core practices that appear critical for building contextual intelligence. As you read these, remember this isn't a massive production – another burden on top of your 'real' work, but rather a guide to more carefully structuring activities you probably already do and are committing to doing them a little more often:

- The willingness and clarity to re-engage with experiences
- Identifying assumptions and emotions
- Pattern recognition
- Reframing and synthesis
- Application

BUILDING CONTEXTUAL INTELLIGENCE – FIVE CORE PRACTICES

The Willingness and Clarity to Re-engage with Experiences

This means, in the first instance, openly engaging with new experiences and seeing all of them as potentially meaningful. For a first step, this seems obvious, but remember the daydreaming child in my previous example. A surprising number of us, from child to adult, arrive at potentially transformative experiences, content – if not committed – to being physically present but otherwise absent.

Building contextual intelligence includes purposefully revisiting your experiences – not just those that went well, but also those that confused, frustrated or surprised you: Replaying a recent event in your mind, rewatching a video or re-reading your notes with objective curiosity, and perhaps some questions like this in mind:

- What made this moment/lesson/interaction stand out?
- What details do I now notice that I might have overlooked the first time?
- What new connections have I made by revisiting this?

Identifying Assumptions and Emotions

As you review the 'what' of the experience – whether sitting in a structured learning opportunity or revisiting a recent experience, you should try to understand the underlying beliefs, emotions and 'knee-jerk' or triggered responses. Contextual intelligence demands an honest audit of your internal filters. Every experience is coloured by what we believe, fear or expect.

- What did I assume to be true in this situation – about others, myself or 'how things work'?
- What emotions came up at the time, and what emotions come up now as I revisit it?
- What part of me and how I see the world felt most seen, enhanced or challenged by this information?

Pattern Recognition

This is the part where you purposefully connect the insights gained through the previous stages with other existing knowledge to identify recurring themes.

You are not expected to be a magician here – the process for me is a lot less like knowing the potential connections, than grabbing an insight, like a puzzle piece and pushing it next to another to see if a picture is made. If not, I don't despair. I try again, and when fatigued by the process, rather than frustratedly throwing the piece behind a bit of mental furniture, I add it to the box, knowing it'll be there when I find another potential match.

Application isn't always immediate. Sometimes it's about placing this insight somewhere accessible in your mental toolkit, even if you don't yet know what for. But remember that building contextual intelligence means regularly challenging old conclusions, updating your mental models, and remaining open to complexity.

Questions like this can help place the puzzle pieces:

- Where else have I felt or acted like this, even if the context differed?
- Is this part of a larger pattern I've noticed before?
- Am I working on anything now that could relate to this and enhance my understanding of my peers?
- Which recurring experiences, feelings, reactions or themes keep showing up, even when I'm not looking for them?
- What remains unexplained – and why might that matter?

Reframing and Synthesis

New insights are powerful only when they are integrated into our existing mental frameworks. When I find pieces that fit together, old and new experiences that align, I consider:

- What does this mean for my understanding of [the topic or me]?
- What else is missing?
- What new sparks of ideas are emerging from looking at this new combination?
- What am I now more aware of as a blind spot or missing piece?

Application

Contextual intelligence becomes most visible when it shapes real-world action. It's not endless reflection, but practical impact. Quite simply, it's spending a little time imagining:

- Where might this matter in my context (work or elsewhere)?
- How might this change how I respond, question, or lead?
- Who else might benefit from knowing what I've learned and why, not as a lesson, but as a gift?
- How will I communicate my insights clearly?

I want to share an example of an experience with a reflective integration process I found particularly poignant. Until recently, I lived in Covent Garden and, under sufferance, I went to the gym a couple of times a week. After arriving at 06:00, and spending an hour with my trainer, I would leave, grab a snack from the ridiculously priced 'health bar' and head home, knowing I would pass a coffee shop just in time for it to open. I was often their first customer and in the midst of opening up, I realised I was – and not in an unpleasant way – invisible to them.

Two young men were working, and both spoke English as a second language. From their accents, neither spoke the same first language, so they talked to each other in English as they made my coffee.

I listen in. I know that isn't polite, but it was compelling. Two immigrants were talking about what they wanted to achieve in life while a coffee grinder bellowed. One telling the other how much they had to offer the world, 'if only people could *really* see us'.

One placed a steam wand into milk and mulled that statement while the other wiped down a surface.

When he stopped steaming the milk for my coffee, he tapped it rhythmically as he said in return, 'but how can they see us? When they look at us, they see only *this*'.

He pointed up and down at first, him and then his colleague.

I can't tell which part of his identity he was referring to – the coffee-stained apron or some other part of them that only they knew.

But neither spoke again, in the short minute before one popped a lid on my coffee and manufactured a smile as he handed it to me. He didn't make eye contact at first, but I held in place long enough to do just that, nod at them both and leave.

This experience inhabited me for the remaining five minutes of my walk home – I didn't know why it was so profound, but as the sun rose over London, I rewatched it again and again.

I considered the first embarrassing reason for the experience being profound. I had clearly assumed something I had not acknowledged consciously and didn't like about me: young people working in coffee shops are incapable of being thoughtful enough for me to notice.

It was striking because very few times have I understood quite so clearly that I stereotype so harshly. It was chastening and made me wonder where else I was making this mistake; my mind leapt back to an interaction with a client that didn't go so well, and I knew I had contributed to that with my approach and underestimation of them.

But the walk back was dominated by one idea: that there were so many ways I could use this experience. I knew I wanted to tell the audiences I speak to, even as I hadn't completely understood the various lessons in this parable-like experience.

Five minutes. In a coffee shop in Soho. And I still feel grateful for that experience now. Even revisiting this memory now has inspired more thoughts and connections. I am thankful that the primary opportunity it presented has been taken to heart; I am more conscientious about some of the less obvious stereotypes I held.

None of this is to say you can't just bask in the joy of learning for learning's sake. Be open to the experience and then decide to learn what you might from it, but you'll miss opportunities and learn less this way. This process of revisiting experiences is important because it is how we really learn.

In work and school, we encounter bosses and educators who seem confused that we ever forget anything we are told, when the way we learn involves forgetting and revisiting. There's a pervasive myth in education (whether professional or academic) that all good conscientious people learn like this:

Exposure to new information → Absorb new information → Retain new information

When in reality, learning is a reflective process that looks different for most of us, but more like:

Exposure to new information → Mostly Forgetting → Retrieval → Partial Forgetting → Retrieval (Synthesis with connection and utility) → Learning

Whatever your approach to learning, recognise that it isn't a straight line from exposure to mastery and as much as you can't expect that from yourself, ask yourself if you can expect it from your colleagues either.

PILLARS OF LIFELONG LEADERSHIP LEARNING

In a leadership or personal development context, embracing this approach to learning through integrating what you already know with a curiosity for what's new and potentially useful matters because it fuels improved self-awareness. Recognising one's behavioural patterns, blind spots and motivators with a mind to enhancing and amending them is inherently enhancing for our self-awareness. It hones our pattern recognition too. Turning disparate experiences, lessons and events into cohesive insights isn't just informative about the past; it helps you make more informed and effective predictions.

Another advantage is adaptability. Learning not just from the layering of formal education and taught knowledge, but by incorporating varied and new information into familiar neural pathways.

Then there's our judgement – the ability to make more nuanced, balanced and important decisions based on a catalogue of context-rich, lived evidence and learnings that minimise the temptation to make rash decisions and the ability to see up front the predictable and potentially even unintended consequences of our actions.

Some of you will already have voices in your head screaming, 'When am I supposed to make time for this?' But what's taken me this chapter to describe is a process, with practice that runs in parallel and in the spaces between experiences and engagement with others, not formal learning. No extra time required, but as always, with anything I recommend, it'll cost you some energy.

Here are a few last points regarding adding new insights.

Know Your 'Basics'

Many of you will consume a daily diet of what I call the 'basics' – these are the sources I might reliably expect any relatively conscientious person in your position and sector to consume to stay informed.

If you don't know what these are in your sector, find out – you're doing yourself a disservice. These are essential, but they are insufficient for most aspiring to be more than competent.

I will add a list of my 'basics' at the end of this chapter, not because you are all aspiring psychologists, but because my 'basics' might end up being your extras.

Just One Thing

Fundamental and licence or qualification-maintenance continuing professional development (CPD) (usually assigned by a licensing or membership institution), but may also be assigned by your organisation as part of compliance training, are also part of the 'usuals'.

One of the things that bothers me about CPD is that much of our syllabus is often perfunctory and dull when it doesn't need to be.

I had to refresh my fire safety and working from home occupational hazard CPD every year, and I swear it should be repackaged as a sleep aid.

While you can rely on the learning and development you'll receive from the APS Intelligence team to enthral you (I promise!), I have reframed my thinking when I attend or have to take these 'click and quiz'-style compliance exercises.

'Can I grab one valuable thing?'

Not two, not 'a few', just one.

It can be from the content, teaching approach, graphical layout or digital framework. Any one thing makes the exercise a success.

From my fire safety, I grabbed 'dry powder fire extinguishers work on every type of fire'. As I type this, I am looking at one of those extinguishers on the floor beyond my computer screen. I am safer for the training, even as I am not as informed as I might be.

Set Aside Time

Almost everything useful I know now, I learned after my graduate studies. It comes from wonderful interactions with peers, mistakes made with support for learning from them, and other excellent sources I'll talk about later.

You don't need to sit down for hours, or even an hour, to add to your knowledge base. You can learn some things at least, in snippets of time and a set learning syllabus.

Build a daily routine with a discrete time for these snippets.

I wake up and if it's early enough, I'll enjoy the shipping forecast on Radio 4; if not, as is more usual now, I will skip the radio and go straight to my LinkedIn feed and bookmark anything I think is interesting for follow-up or re-read.

I'll check my other socials, too, because I am lucky enough to have followers who contribute great ideas as much as they seek fresh insights.

I have two custom GPT Tasks that produce two pieces of daily content (*Daily Client Insight Briefing* and *Daily Delight Drop*). They are delivered at 06:00 and usually include something short to watch or listen to as I take care of my ablutions. You can see the actual prompts at the end of this chapter.

I set aside time to reflect on my experiences twice a week, but always once. I have a comfortable chair in the corner of my living room that looks over east and south-east London, Canary Wharf and more. A few months ago, the wonderful people at the Dan Lebatard Show (a Miami-based sports and current affairs show with wacky tendencies that I have been an occasional guest on for 30 years) officially named it 'The Pondering Chair'.

It stuck.

So now, at least one weekend morning, I make tea, pour some ice water, sit in the Pondering Chair, watch the sunrise, and bake in the sun (or look through the rain – it's England after all) for as long as the tea is hot and there's water left in the glass. I think about the week just gone: what I learned, how I felt about it and what I will do with what I now know.

I know you'll have people vying for your time, but make some time – one cup of tea's worth of time, from dry tea leaves to empty cup – to reflect and you'll grow as a learning leader.

Where snippets won't do, look around at available one-hour short sessions delivered by your licensing or other membership body and add them to your diary. Check out sites like Eventbrite, whose recent reorientation has them showing massive numbers of inexpensive to free events.

If you're ambitious, you can also look for the major conferences. For me, this is the British Psychological Society Annual and Division of Occupational Psychology conferences and the Association for Business Psychology Conference to start. I know I won't always be able to attend, but they are in the diary as a reminder to commit if possible. Many are eclipsed by work, but some conferences or shorter online CPD sessions remain this way.

Mix Up Your Sources

Don't just stick to scientific journals. Don't just stick to *Harvard Business Review, MIT Sloan* or *Management Today.*

There are brilliant technical and general knowledge videos, infographics, and more – available from multiple sources – and, importantly, I think, they are free (well, mostly in exchange for your personal information!)

Don't scoff at the power of social media. TikTok has inspired great ideas in me for this book and my coaching – you need to find your tribe, so you aren't inundated with rubbish, but there is fantastic stuff to see if you're patient and purposefully look to follow smart people as well as the latest dance meme. If the algorithm isn't serving you and you've been on it for a while, consider looking at people whose algorithm is more fitting and follow them.

I had a distraught senior leader come to me recently who had found his TikTok algorithm had 'turned all gay' and all he saw was shirtless men. I thought twice about helping him know how the algorithm worked, but I didn't have the heart, so we started him out again with a new login. Let's see how that goes.

I follow a few great content creators on YouTube, but my first exposure to Veritasium hooked me on that platform. After you've finished this chapter, go and watch his video on Luck: https://www.youtube.com/@veritasium

Some social media are less valuable: Twitter – and it will always be Twitter – is a cesspool, but I still follow several researchers, brilliant thinkers, and industry experts there. However, if you want to hear what I am saying, you'll need to go to BlueSky (@johnamaechi.apsintel.com), TikTok (@johnamaechiobe), Instagram (@johnamaechiobe), and LinkedIn (https://www.linkedin.com/in/amaechi/) nowadays.

Share While You Learn

While I haven't been part of an official learning cohort for some time, I am in several unofficial learning cohorts until I join my next Mastermind group. Find people who are interesting and curious, and try some of these:

- *Masterminds:* online format is a peer learning community where a small group of individuals (typically 8–10 people) meet regularly via digital platforms to support each other's professional and personal growth. I facilitate a couple of monthly masterminds, so if you're interested, you're welcome to join that waitlist.
- *Lunch and Learns:* You don't have to wait until your company or organisation creates one – pick a group, eat your lunch, and

have one of you share something you know for the group, and then open to questions. You will have a blast.

- *Speak at Conferences:* You don't have to attend conferences only; you can speak at them. Many conferences have smaller half-hour plenary sessions where you can speak on topics related to the conference theme and in your knowledge sweet spot.
- *Seek a Mentor:* You'll never know until you reach out if that person you admire will respond. First, let me say this:
  - Don't confuse famous with expert.
  - Don't conflate someone being active on social media with them being social!
  - Don't imagine someone you admire will necessarily have the mentoring or coaching skills you seek.
- But if you see someone who intrigues you and you're looking for a mentor, reach out, with a few caveats – don't blind email (or especially DM on socials) if you haven't prepared a script which tells them you aren't trying to waste their time. I'd consider looking at this as a model for approaching them:
  - A bit of backstory.
  - Who are you now?
  - What do you do?
  - What do you want to achieve?
  - Why do you think this person (specifically) can help you?
  - What commitment are you looking for? (One off, monthly or other engagement cadence.)
  - Why YOU? Of all the people who contact them, why you?

Reflection does not transform us independently – what we do with the insights gathered matters. This final section will offer practical ways to weave integrative reflection into your leadership and learning rhythms. You do not need to adopt every idea – instead, think of this as a menu from which to select one or two practices that feel achievable and aligned with your way of working.

Principles into Practice: Making it Real
Building Contextual Intelligence:
Five Core Practices

The Willingness and Clarity to Re-engage with Experiences

- What made this moment/lesson/interaction stand out?
- What details do I now notice that I might have overlooked the first time?
- What new connections have I made by revisiting this?

Identifying Assumptions and Emotions

- What did I assume to be true in this situation – about others, myself, or 'how things work'
- What emotions came up at the time, and what emotions come up now as I revisit it?
- What part of me and how I see the world felt most seen, enhanced or challenged by this information?

Pattern Recognition

- Where else have I felt or acted like this, even if the context differed?
- Is this part of a larger pattern I've noticed before?

- Am I working on anything now that could relate to this and enhance my understanding of my peers?
- Which recurring experiences, feelings, reactions or themes keep showing up, even when I'm not looking for them?
- What remains unexplained – and why might that matter?

Reframing and Synthesis

- What does this mean for my understanding of [the topic or me]?
- What else is missing?
- What new sparks of ideas are emerging from looking at this new combination?
- What am I now more aware of as a blind spot or missing piece?

Application

- Where might this matter in my context (work or elsewhere)?
- How might this change how I respond, question or lead?
- Who else might benefit from knowing what I've learned and why, not as a lesson, but as a gift?
- How will I clearly communicate my insights?

Are You Covering the 'Basics'?

Do you read or engage, at roughly the same cadence, with the same materials as other people in your sector and role?

(Continued)

If you don't know, ask colleagues to share one way they are staying current and ahead of the curve regarding professional development and cutting-edge insight.

Ensure you aren't caught out by not knowing something that a brief headline from an obvious publication could have told you.

Lots of people curate lists of 'basics' for their industries, so keep an eye out, especially on LinkedIn.

Invisible Observer Exercise

At the end of each working week, write down one moment where you were an 'invisible observer' – witnessing something not meant for you, but not secret – something small but telling.

Without judgement, write briefly:

- Describe the situation and context.
- What made you pay attention?
- What assumptions might you have made initially?
- What surfaced emotionally when you witnessed it?
- What does revisiting it suggest about your leadership or personal tendencies?
- After a month, revisit all your 'invisible moments' and look for emerging patterns.

Technology-Assisted Learning and Reflection

Use AI tasks in GPT or similar to create relevant daily snippets to read or listen to every morning that will help you learn something new and applicable to work, and help you learn something new and delightful, just for you. Prompts for both these are at the end of this chapter.

Other technology-assisted reflection: Self-tracking technology and apps can help you monitor various aspects of your life and provide data for reflection. However, it is important to focus on meaningful insights rather than getting caught up in data collection alone.

I wear a Whoop band for sleep and longitudinal insights and an Apple Watch for exercise. I am not endorsed by either, and I know others might suit you better, but Whoop, for example, does help me track my sleep and stress because it's always on.

They both have given me insights, but I recently noticed a dramatic insight about my response to work. For example, whether delivering a speech in person or virtually, my heart rate dips to at or below my resting rate as I deliver, then rises slightly when I begin the Q&A before falling back to my resting rate while I respond to questions. Then, when I end, my heart rate spikes into zone 4. If I'm virtual, this spike is short-lived, as usually in a matter of minutes, I will either be preparing for or entering another client engagement. So the virtual spike and the associated physiological changes – sweating, especially – may last for 60 seconds to a few minutes, until I refocus on the next task.

(Continued)

But if I am in person, especially when I meet and greet people or enter a 'networking' environment, my heart rate spikes and stays high, sometimes for 30–40 minutes, leaving me a sweaty mess.

We mustn't get caught up in the data capture elements alone; instead, we must consider what this means for our operation. I have used it to change how I schedule virtual events, removing most back-to-backs to leave time for rebalancing. In person, my 'rider' (the document that details technical and hospitality requirements for an event) requests a private room, so I can have a space to recover and de-sweat, away from prying eyes!

Some of you are already using the data you've gathered, even if it's just a nebulous feeling of stress or needing to escape a loud workspace. It's the headphones you wear in open-plan offices, the remote bench outside or on the grounds of your workplace where you know you can find solitude.

Even those who wonder why so many don't bring food to work 'because it's cheaper' but instead head out to buy a sandwich or snack – part of it may be variety or ease, but it's also a way to guarantee a venue change, even if it's an anonymous queue of people, where they are able, perhaps for the first time that day, to put headphones in, chat to a loved one, listen to a podcast or music, or as many do, put headphones in with nothing playing but their own thoughts.

What patterns have you spotted relating to your heart rate, sleeping patterns, sleep or waking hours, and what does that suggest for changes to your operation?

My 'Basics'

Here are some of the 'basics' I rely on to stay connected to the broader world of ideas and leadership practice. You do not need to consume them all, but building your foundation is essential. Some of these are paywalled, but nearly all the sites that are paywalled offer newsletters that add quick value. Lastly, I have not included any of the specialist memberships where you must be, for example, a qualified psychologist or HR professional in the United Kingdom and/or United States to access their resources.

https://www.statista.com – I get the daily newsletter highlighting interesting stats on topical subjects, and a deeper dive is available.

https://www.theneurondaily.com – weekly newsletter on technology, especially applications and misapplications of generative AI.

https://www.tortoisemedia.com – so called 'slow news' with in-depth stories – I am an early subscriber, but there are free stories and a 'sense maker' newsletter.

https://hbr.org – only three articles a month, but you can access the numerous newsletters https://hbr.org/email-newsletters and their 'reading list' https://hbr.org/reading-lists.

(Continued)

https://mbrjournal.com – built a few years ago as an
alternative to HBR (and perhaps a more credible
academic source), but only the 2021 digital versions are free.

https://www.researchgate.net – lots of new and yet-to-
be-published research and open-source (free)
research.)

https://www.elsevier.com/en-gb/search-results?labels=
journals – journals and books to access – clicking the
'open access' tab will filter out anything you can't
access in full. But you can often get a lot of information
just from the abstract!

https://www.hr-brew.com/r?kid=03f3c983 – I read this
every day – workplace people, culture and leadership
issues and a bit of a sense of humour too! (This link is a
referral link for me, but I don't get anything for it other
than seeing how many people subscribe based on my
referral, because the 'free coffee cup' is unavailable to
people outside the United States!)

https://www.mckinsey.com/featured-insights/the-daily-read–
McKinsey Daily read (I also subscribe to their insights
hub).

https://www.managers.org.uk/knowledge-and-insights/ –
most of these are free to access.

https://www.ft.com – front page – every day.

https://www.ft.com/newsletters – subscribe to the free newsletters related to your client sectors or interest areas.

https://www.bbc.co.uk/programmes/m0017cq4 – join BBC iPlayer and subscribe to this show (if you aren't up at 06:00 and listen to it): 06:07 is about when the paper review starts, listen to headlines for about 3–4 minutes; business news at 06:15 normally for 5–8 mins. You can listen up to four times the speed, which is what I do if I don't catch it live.

https://www.retailbrew.com/r?kid=03f3c983 – This is Retail Brew, not the same as the Morning Brew newsletter, but it can also be subscribed to Morning Brew!

https://www.cbinsights.com/newsletter/ – business insights and topical matters

https://hbr.org/email-newsletters – management tip of the day (our clients will have seen these); Leadership; The Daily Alert

https://fs.blog/newsletter/

https://www.hrdive.com/signup – daily dive; talent daily.

Chat GPT Prompts

Here is the simple prompt for my Daily Client Insight Briefing:
You are an analyst for APS Intelligence Ltd, a London-based psychological leadership and culture consultancy founded by

(Continued)

Professor John Amaechi. Each weekday at 06:00 UK time, you will deliver a concise 'Daily Client Insight Brief' that:

1. Scans EU and UK news, policy updates and business events that could influence senior leaders in large, complex organisations (e.g. FTSE- or Fortune-listed).
2. Note any relevant US developments or stories with potential knock-on effects for UK/EU leadership, culture or people strategy.
3. Summarises in three or four crisp bullet-point sections ('UK', 'EU', 'US'), each with a clear implication for leadership or culture advisory.
4. Follows APSI style: British English spelling, bold and credible tone, no clichés or coaching jargon, and non-patronising language.
5. It is delivered both as a brief in the chat and as a downloadable Word document (with an accompanying visual dashboard).

Audience: Busy senior executives who want clear, evidence-led intelligence to provoke reflection, spark strategic conversations and shape demand for APSI's services.

Your task: Search for EU/UK events, capture US influences, draw out the leadership-culture implications, and package it for immediate use by John Amaechi and the APS Intelligence team.

Here is the prompt I am using to create my *Daily Delight* newsletter. Feel free to amend or dissect it to create something delightful for you daily. I still have some problems with broken links, but the newsletter is a lovely way to start or end the day, and obviously, amend as fits your personality.

John Amaechi's Daily Delight *(Latest Version)*

Generate a 'Daily Delight' drop, explicitly curated for John Amaechi and delivered every weekday at 06:00 UK time and every weekend day at 09:00 UK time.

Each edition must intrigue, uplift or gently provoke thought – a reflective, non-business companion that may be consumed later in the day.

Content should evoke awe, beauty, weirdness or poignancy, *never* descending into gloom or cynicism.

Each edition should contain a curated mix (not a fixed structure) drawn from the following:

- A great quote or very short passage – literary, philosophical, scientific, or surprising – from any discipline, including those far outside psychology.
- One musical recommendation from the 1980s (UK, US, or global) including originals, revivals, or re-recordings. Include an Apple Music link that has been thoroughly verified.

(Continued)

- An insight, phrase, or proverb from the African diaspora – prioritising historically resonant, non-Christian indigenous Igbo wisdom where possible.
- Optional: a beautiful or unusual short story, artwork, podcast snippet, or philosophical curiosity.

Tone and Curation Guidelines:

- No American sports.
- Cultural references should skew global and diasporic – including queer, Black and cross-cultural lenses.
- No clichés or overly sentimental content – wonder and elegance over platitudes.
- Must be fully compatible with the Apple ecosystem (Apple Music, Apple Podcasts, etc.).
- Maximum reading time: Five minutes.
- Spelling must be British English. Never use ampersands ('and' only).

Goal:

Offer John a refreshing, high-quality mosaic of insights and aesthetic pleasures that nourish his *Library of Experiences*, with enough texture to intrigue, but light enough to lift.

Contextual intelligence is not built by accident – it is shaped moment by moment by those willing to learn, connect, and act deliberately. You will not regret making it your new everyday practice. Give it a go!

CHAPTER TEN

ENABLING OTHERS' GROWTH

IT'S NOT MAGIC. . . IT'S EFFORT AND INTENTION

conclude this book with a chapter on enabling growth in others. I will provide approaches for leaders to foster growth in their teams and for any individual to use to inspire another, to help them develop their own 'libraries of experiences' and a unique and authentic voice.

Being a leader, named or unnamed, is not just about being right or decisive or being seen as the expert in the room. It is about creating environments where others can think, feel and grow with clarity and confidence. Enabling others' growth is not a magical ability but a deliberate practice of careful observation, encouragement, precision and thoughtfully robust challenge. This chapter explores how leaders can build that practice with intention and skill.

Michelle's research commented on my approach to observing others, which might be worth considering for your practice. While these practices might be familiar in coaching or even some therapeutic fields, using them is not about 'being a therapist' as much as being a quality leader in an increasingly unkind world. You will see the word 'client' here as I think of this in the context of my coaching work with senior executives, but substitute in 'colleague', 'direct report' partner or child and you'll find these insights helpful.

OBSERVING OTHERS: READING THE SIGNALS OF GROWTH AND STRUGGLE

I especially look out for cognitive dissonance in others. This is not just between what they say and how they've acted in the past or have stated they plan to act in the future, but between body language and words in the moment.

I cannot tell you how often I have heard somebody describe their 'excitement' about a new role or project while looking at their face and body, shrugging, and then sighing fretfully and in unison. I am unsure if it's the manifestation movement (something I am wildly against in the simplistic *Field of Dreams* way it is presented), but the 'if you build it, they will come' turns out not to be very viable without some fairly large caveats – one early one is believing what you say when you say it.

A surprising number of people don't seem to know that they don't believe the things they regularly say. When observing others in a way designed to support and help them grow, you mustn't jump to 'you're a liar!' when you first spot incongruences. My experience is that basic lying is the rarest of reasons for this kind of incongruence. Many other chapters deal with the more prescient reasons, a lack of self-knowledge, self-assurance, and so on.

Instead, based on your observation, consider how you can centre the confusion borne of the incongruence you witness in *yourself*, as internal confusion rather than jabbing your observational stick into the eye of their dissonance. In my example, I didn't just say, 'You don't believe that!' when I am told someone's 'excited' about some opportunity. Instead, I muse about what I might be misunderstanding. I am unequivocal about what I saw, so I don't provide the chance to pretend I didn't see and hear what I did. Instead, I leave openings for refinement and new information.

'I didn't hear as much excitement as expected when you said that. Am I missing something?'

I can't tell you what started me looking at this, but whether an expectation bias or not, I see this whenever I watch people, whether prime ministers talking about the 'confidence' they have in a cabinet member who is subsequently sacked the next day or young people talking about themselves, their plans and their hopes for their lives.

I would point out that just because you spot an incongruence that irritates you doesn't give you the right to scratch that itch.

It can feel like an assault on people when there are gaps between what they say and their beliefs in those words or how they behave, so you don't start a conversation about these gaps just because they irritate you. There's a process for tightening these gaps. While people can have instant revelations, most require ongoing conversations with thoughtful, but robust challenges to see change happen and grow past the dissonance. If you're not up for that, perhaps you're not the person to kick that process off.

A good plan for managing the observations of discrepancies is:

- Contextualise confusion from witnessed discrepancies in yourself.
- Ask for clarification for yourself, rather than intimate the person is themselves confused, dissonant or, worse still, a liar.
- Give people the opportunity to refine or add new information that closes the dissonance gap.
- Observe these changes without judgement, but notice them overtly and how they differ from what was initially said.
- Commit to ongoing contact where you remember previous interactions.

The last point here is a place I see leaders screw up all the time – opening up a conversation with some depth, that may challenge them, and then doing no work to create (at least) a mental record of the conversation. No one wants to start from square one every time they meet, so if you see some shift in the gap, be prepared to remember it for the person and keep track of overall changes. Much like with weight loss, it happens over time, so the only way you can know is when you meet someone who reminds you how much weight you've lost – or how much closer aligned your words and deeds are now than previously.

Remember that spotting dissonance is not about exposing weakness. It is about identifying where an individual's inner narrative and external expression are misaligned, offering a unique opportunity for targeted support, confidence building, and clearer goal setting. Growth often starts where someone feels the tension between what they say and what they genuinely believe.

Next, I look for patterns between the experiences clients express and those I have seen in others. There isn't one part of me that thinks 'all people are the same', but as explained in the last chapter, it can provide new insights when a new piece of information is added to an existing one. Sometimes the starting state of one client will resemble that of another. I keep the other client's journey playing like a background track at a diner, not loud enough to get in the way of conversation, but just enough to break into my consciousness during a lull. When I notice patterns, it allows me to make the occasional and judicious, intuitive leap, where I reach a conclusion or gain understanding without going through conscious, sequential reasoning steps.

Going through the process of your distinct pattern is essential, so I employ this mostly when people find themselves unexpectedly stuck, to give them a nudge back on track.

I also use it to highlight unintentional or under-considered consequences of a course of action I've witnessed before. When you're as old as I am, there are surprisingly niche scenarios in which I have almost identical previous clients whose paths have highlighted at least some of the potholes and pitfalls, but if you're just getting started, there will be fewer patterns to recall. Just give it time:

- Notice when a client's current situation faintly echoes another's journey, without assuming identical outcomes.
- Use remembered patterns to prompt exploration: 'I've seen others find that. . . does that resonate for you?'
- Recognise patterns highlighting hidden risks or opportunities that might not yet be visible to the client.
- Resist the urge to 'prescribe' solutions based on pattern familiarity – use patterns to generate better questions, not shortcuts.

Pattern recognition allows leaders to accelerate others' insight without robbing them of the opportunity to own the pain and triumph of their discovery. It turns quiet intuition into a tool for curiosity and careful prompting, rather than lazy stereotyping.

Next, I am always looking for unexpected difficulties coaching clients have in answering simple questions (especially about themselves). This includes overly long pauses (10 seconds or more), stumbling and restarting a response multiple times, or rapid speech that differs from the regular cadence.

I recognise that nerves play some part in people's non-optimal interpersonal interactions, but each of these elements helps me ask new questions – for example, not being able to answer questions about themselves could be a sign that a client doesn't know themselves very well, or it can be an inability to reframe the response they think is real into an appropriate response for the person in front of them. Part of the reason it's so key not to rush to judgement is that neither of those makes this person 'bad', but both require different questions to begin to tease out some insight for them.

While long pauses – and I am the king of long pauses and use them liberally, but never because I don't know an answer; I usually just say 'I don't know' after a moment's consideration! – can be about nerves, they are more often a product of constructing an answer that has not been previously considered. This may mean someone is generally less introspective or simply underprepared in an interview format.

Restarting responses is very often a product of starting to respond before thoughts in one's head have been turned into a cogent answer. My usual advice when talking to people doing this is to slow down and take more time up front so you can 'buffer' more of your response before you kick off.

Please believe me when I say this has nothing to do with speech impediments or cultural quirks, even as they may impact an individual's perception. I am interested in supporting people for success in a world where many jump to conclusions and judgement far too quickly, so I feel it's a responsibility to point out and attempt to change, where practical, underdeveloped skills that impact how clients are seen and heard.

A point that regularly raises the heat in coaching conversations with me is when answers are purposefully vague, when the client avoids the question I ask, or when the client doesn't attempt an answer at all.

All the people I work with are at least 'book smart', but it's once a week at least where I find myself playing rhetorical games with people I am attempting to support, where they claim not to understand standard conventions or basic concepts; those people who respond when I ask, 'Did you meet the deadline?' with 'When you say, "meet" what do you mean?'

I admit, it's one of the interchanges that makes my ears hot when I notice it beginning.

I also see clients do this when answering an adjacent question, sometimes even saying 'I think the question that's more important is. . .' usually in more detail than required, rather than the specific question I asked.

The last kind of question avoidance is when people attack the questions themselves. I write surveys for clients all the time, so I know how to construct a decent question that follows the BRUSO (Brief, Relevant, Unambiguous, Specific and Objective) rules,[1] but it is as consistent as the sun rising that someone I speak to will focus all their mental energy on the question rather than the answer.

For all this, and as frustrating as it may be, it's our job as people who want to enable growth in others to point out avoidance or unexpected gaps in self-knowledge, and support them to find their answers and their voice.

- Pauses may indicate a need for time to connect emotion to language. Allow space rather than rushing to fill silence.
- Stumbling and restarting suggest that ideas have not yet crystallised. Slow the pace; encourage the client to gather thoughts fully before speaking.
- Rapid speech can signal anxiety, fear of judgement, or unchecked internal scripts. Gentle prompting to breathe and refocus can restore clarity.

For vague, avoidant or deflective responses, consider the following:

- Gently but firmly return to the original question when avoidance is spotted: 'Let's return to what I asked for a moment. . .'
- When deflection occurs, name it lightly: 'That's an interesting perspective – and I still wonder about [restate question]'.
- If the question itself is attacked, reinforce purpose: 'The question's purpose is to understand your experience, let's avoid debating semantics. . .'.

Avoidance behaviours are not necessarily signs of incompetence or impertinence – they often signal discomfort, fear of judgement or internalised perfectionism. Addressing avoidance is not about 'winning' but helping the individual feel safe enough to confront uncertainty honestly.

When individuals struggle to answer, they often reveal where self-knowledge is still forming. Leaders who respond with patience and curiosity, not impatience, personal embarrassment or intentional humiliation, help create the conditions for authentic self-awareness to grow.

BOOSTING CONFIDENCE: NORMALISING, AFFIRMING AND REFRAMING GAPS

I revel in the opportunity to reassure people who, sometimes for decades, haven't realised that their experiences, feelings and thoughts are 'normal'. The task of assuaging fears in clients and colleagues that they're responding irrationally is rife right now – whether they've been overlooked for a promotion, bullied at work or had their name misremembered (and mispronounced when remembered), even after seven years of working for the same boss (true story!).

There are so many people, it appears to me, who wander this world, plagued by concerns that any number of people in their orbit could have dissuaded them from if they'd cared to notice and share their own similar journey from misunderstanding to grounded reality.

In times of transformation, please do not underestimate the number of people around you who are slowed, cowed and stunted by concerns about how they think and feel under duress. These concerns can cause otherwise driven and ambitious people to seize up without intervention.

- Acknowledge emotional reactions as normal responses to abnormal or complex conditions.

- Name experiences empathetically: 'It's understandable you felt unseen/ attacked/ humiliated/ excited, etc. after that experience'.
- Share a parallel story (briefly) to normalise, but not hijack, the conversation.
- Reassure without trivialising: validate both the feeling and the impact.
- Emphasise that professional growth often begins with recognising that difficult reactions are not signs of weakness, but signals for needed change.
- Don't lie that reactions would be considered normal if they wouldn't be.

Normalising emotions is not about coddling. It reactivates stalled ambition, protects confidence under strain, and prevents harmful internalisation of systemic issues as personal failures. Leaders who normalise without diminishing the people they address strengthen adaptive coping mechanisms and promote sustained engagement in their work.

As I talk to people, insecurities often appear quickly, and beyond reassurance now, I use the techniques and approach described in Chapter Five to turn perceived 'gaps' into a platform for growth. I won't say much more here, but returning to that chapter will fully explain this approach.

I am not a warm and fuzzy psychologist; I am not effusive with (collegial) love or compliments when with peers or clients, but I enjoy giving compliments that matter.

I enjoy giving compliments that help people see that I was paying attention, see their effort and incisiveness, where present, and the impact on the development of the conversation and their personal and professional growth.

My approach follows a pattern.

- Notice the 'small wins' – consistency, thoughtfulness or subtle progress.
- Reward effort, learning processes and strategic risk-taking, not just outcomes.
- Be granular and precise about what you are complimenting and why it matters.
- Tie positive observations explicitly to personal or shared goals.
- Gently but firmly resist deflections or minimisations – ensure the compliment lands fully.

Precision in praise builds self-awareness. Vague compliments wash over people and can appear especially vacuous if the criticism they receive is more granular; precise feedback helps individuals internalise their strengths and replicate them consciously. Leaders who celebrate the good things, done well, teach others what matters.

It hurts me to see remarkable people who don't see themselves as such. Worse still, when people have pinned their sense of self-worth to their occupation and their role isn't offering what it once did or should, or when they are struggling to adapt to a new role, they lose their sense of self.

When I work with transitioning athletes, one of the first and most difficult things I do is discuss disentangling what a person does (and how well they do it) from their identity.

Even for us, who are not (or are no longer) professional athletes, it's not hyperbole to say that in an age of constant change and transformation to job roles, professions and entire job sectors, there's little more dangerous for a working-age person than having their occupation become their definition.

I want people to see their self-worth. Some of it concerns knowing that self-worth, when resolute, bolsters people and provides a sense of inner stability in a storm.

However, some of it is less philanthropic than prophylactic. When I look at the world, in politics, academia and workplaces, I recognise that people lack a steadfast sense of self-worth, they become troubled, and when powerful enough, occupying positions of influence, that 'troubled' becomes 'troublesome' for everyone else.[2]

- Encourage conversations about personal values, not just professional achievements.
- Help clients identify enduring traits (e.g., 'I am resilient' or 'I am thoughtful') separate from job titles.
- Support the development of identity anchors (elements of themselves that are valuable regardless of work context) that are portable across careers.
- Challenge harmful narratives that equate job status with personal worth.

Studies show that individuals with broader, multifaceted self-concepts are more resilient during role transitions and career shocks.[3] When self-worth is tethered too tightly to a role, any change becomes a threat rather than an opportunity. Leaders who help others build identity resilience create individuals who can evolve, not just survive.

SHARPENING THINKING: PRECISION, SPECIFICITY AND OWNERSHIP

I love this part. Those of you who are agile and active listeners will too. It is the idea that you listen to people and where you hear generalisations, euphemisms, metaphors, platitudes or sophistry, you can gently jump in and push them for specifics, clearer examples and more definitive language to explain their experience and what they mean you to understand.

I often ask why people use the turn of phrase they do.

One coaching client of mine was interpersonally warm when we spoke, but used the language of computers and machinery when he talked about how he felt and thought – 'wrench in my gears' – and talked about his mind as a computer. I asked him about it, and although everyone around him was aware of this consistent turn of phrase and thought of him as an efficient transactional computer rather than a human being in part because of it, he had no clue.

Because I know that people get into patterns that become so familiar they stop recognising them, I sometimes need to demonstrate how to sharpen examples and expressions. Instead of, or as well as, asking them for clarity, I reframe and reflect what others say with helpful and clarifying changes, or I add context that they've either missed or taken for granted as they speak, that might change, sometimes quite radically, the implications or tone of what they say.

This is another area where the library of experiences comes in handy. When people speak (and stay unclenched!), complementary examples to illustrate or clarify their points seem to bubble to the surface, ready to be deployed to provide context or colour to someone's words and thoughts. And because I have taken experiences from so many sectors over the years, I can usually find an example that people can visualise happening in reality, rather than apocryphally, ensuring my audience, whether one or many, can relate to the content I share.

I always check, 'Does that make sense?', 'Was that the kind of thing you were talking about?' or 'Does that more accurately describe what you were thinking?'

It's our job as leaders to push for the underlying meaning. It's not always necessary to do this, but when we know someone is saying one thing and feeling or thinking another, it's in our best interest to reject the mask and ask what's going on underneath.

- Gently challenge generalisations: ask for one real-world example.
- Notice habitual metaphors and probe their implications.
- Reflect reworded summaries back to the individual to sharpen meaning.
- Use sector-agnostic or sector-specific analogies to ground vague descriptions.
- When you reframe or expand, confirm clarity by asking: 'Does this describe what you were trying to express?'

Language both reflects and shapes thought. By sharpening language, leaders help others hone their thinking, making implicit ideas explicit, and bringing hidden assumptions into conscious choice.

MODELLING REFLECTIVE LEADERSHIP: BEING THE EXAMPLE OTHERS CAN FOLLOW

I broadly encourage, demonstrate and reward reflections and acute personal observations. There is literally a whole chapter on this, but it is essential for growth, so I'd add one nuanced piece here for coaches and leaders with direct reports.

Although how other people see you shouldn't be all that informs who you are to yourself, how you are seen by others, especially at work, can radically and negatively impact how and if you progress.

I regularly, and as gently as possible, challenge people on how they think they are seen by others, not to shift chameleon-like into compliance, but to reflect on how others perceive them will impact what they want to achieve in that or other environments and consider whether and how it's worth changing anything they do to ameliorate a negative or augment a positive perception. The caustic impact of perception means this is one of the few areas where I am willing to give action planning advice after articulating my perceptions from my and their stakeholders' perspectives.

- Regularly articulate your own reflections during conversations: 'Something I'm noticing about myself is. . .'
- Invite others to explore perception versus intention without defensiveness: 'How do you think that came across?'
- Support action planning based on reflection: 'What might you adjust next time based on what you now see?'

Leaders who demonstrate and reward reflection make it safer for others to step back from instinct, habit and reflexive responses. Reflection normalises adaptation, the cornerstone of personal and professional growth.

PHYSICAL PATTERNS

Lastly, I want to talk about my physical patterns. I acknowledge that these are a function of my size (if you've got this far without realising I am huge, bravo.) But I mention these patterns here for one reason. They apply to you, too.

If you're a named leader or someone without a management title, but imbued with status, credibility, or even coolness for some other reason, then you, too, are a Giant.

If none of those apply to you, you're not scot-free. To reiterate something I said at the beginning of this book, everyone is a Giant to someone.

Please consider these physical patterns as ways to better engage with and enable growth through challenging times and interpersonal tensions.

A Gentle Tone of Voice

A giant's whisper is a regular-sized person's shout. To enable someone's growth is always to be cognizant of how you can have a deleterious impact beyond 'saying the wrong thing'.

I am fortunate to be endowed with a decent voice – that some say is soporific, but how I use it is entirely intentional, even, and perhaps especially when it sounds completely spontaneous or unplanned.

Pause to Listen, Emphasise and Think

I speak with lots of pauses. Whether you are listening to this on Audible or with my voice in your head, that will have come across. When I speak to people, I use technology (the mute button) and restraint to grant people space to talk without treading all over their words, and I pause to think in between to ensure enough of my thoughts are buffered into my mind to say precisely what I mean. I also pause to emphasise, both within my sentences and between ideas I am sharing. Showing we are listening with due care, that we think other people are important enough to consider our words carefully and take the time to *really* land essential points, is a path to supporting optimal connection and growth.

Minimal Body Movement

Big people who move quickly are frightening. The 'big, wavey arms thing' that some bosses and public speakers do is reserved for non-giants only – if you're not careful, you'll break someone's nose. Let's face it, even if a person you hope to influence is only slightly concerned about a broken nose around you, growth is probably demoted as a priority for self-preservation!

- Use a warm, measured tone of voice intentionally to reduce perceived threat.
- Employ deliberate pauses to give weight to important ideas and allow others space to think.
- Minimise large, rapid movements, especially when physically larger or higher-status, to avoid overwhelming or distracting others.

Physical presence can either invite or inhibit growth. Leaders who moderate their physical signals thoughtfully create safer environments for reflection, challenge, and honest conversation.

Principles into Practice: Making it Real

Noticing where growth is possible – in someone's language, confidence, self-perception, or ability to reflect – is only the beginning. What matters most is what we choose to do with what we notice. The following practices help you turn careful observation into deliberate, practical support for others' development. You do not need to do them all at once. Please select one or two that resonate, weave them into your rhythm, and let consistent action do what magic never could.

(Continued)

Refine Your Observation Practice

Tool: The 'What I Heard' Check-In

After a section of a critical conversation (whether a feedback session, planning meeting, or development dialogue), pause and say:

> 'Let me tell you what I heard you say and what I think matters most. You tell me what I got right, what I missed, and what needs refining.'

> Remember, each observation is a chance to deepen your understanding, not to catch others out.

Tool: Language Upgrade Challenge

Keep a running note of vague, euphemistic or jargon-heavy phrases you hear in meetings or conversations (including your own) for a week.

At the end of the week, choose three and rewrite them clearly, e.g.:

- 'Going forward, we should synergise efforts' → 'Next week, Helen and I will meet to combine our marketing and sales data'.
- If you are a leader, spend a week using the new clarity in meetings and watch for any differential use of jargon over time.
- After this, inform the team about your attempt to reduce jargon and encourage its elimination.

Tool: Reflective Praise Letter

Once per quarter, write a brief (less than 250-word) 'praise letter' to someone you lead, mentor or admire professionally:

- Focus on *one specific growth moment* you observed.
- Describe *how it mattered* to the person, the team or the broader mission.
- Express gratitude for their effort and insight.
- (Remember this can be life-changing for the recipient, even if you aren't senior.)

Enabling growth in others is not a final achievement but a daily discipline. It is embedded in how we listen, challenge, affirm and create spaces for others to think more clearly and act more purposefully.

Leadership is not magic – it is the accumulated effect of thousands of small, deliberate choices. As you leave the structured path of these chapters, it is time to consider how you can continue the work in the unpredictable, imperfect reality of your own life.

As you step beyond the structured lessons of this book, there is only one real question left: What will you do with what you now know?

Summary

1. Refine Your Observation Practice

- Listen for incongruence between words, tone and body language without rushing to judgement.

(Continued)

- Notice patterns across conversations that may hint at hidden obstacles or strengths.
- Pay attention to how people answer questions – pauses, stumbling or vagueness often signal growth opportunities.

Each observation is a chance to deepen your understanding, not to catch others out.

2. Normalise, Affirm and Reframe with Precision

- Name difficult feelings as valid responses, especially during pressure or change.
- Offer precise, granular compliments that reward effort, thoughtfulness or growth, not just outcomes.
- Help individuals see perceived gaps as invitations to learn, not indictments of character or competence.

Confidence grows strongest where people feel seen clearly and encouraged thoughtfully.

3. Sharpen Language to Sharpen Thinking

- Push gently for specifics when you hear generalisations, metaphors or vagueness.
- Reflect clearer versions of others' ideas back to them, ensuring they recognise and own their strengths.
- Use accessible analogies or examples to ground abstract ideas in reality.

Sharper language builds sharper self-awareness – and better decisions.

4. Model Reflection Openly

- Share your own evolving reflections aloud during conversations.
- Encourage exploration of how individuals are perceived, and where necessary, support action to align perception and intention.
- Normalise revision and reconsideration as marks of strength, not signs of weakness.

Leaders who model reflection permit others to think more deeply, not just perform better.

5. Manage Your Physical Presence

- Use a warm, measured tone and deliberate pacing to foster a safe environment for exploration.
- Pause meaningfully – before responding, between ideas and to emphasise important points.
- Minimise large, abrupt movements, especially when your status or physicality could unintentionally intimidate.

Physical presence speaks loudly. Use it to invite growth, not inhibit it.

EPILOGUE
IT'S NOT MAGIC. . . IT'S YOU

In almost every era, depending on your perspective, a person could claim, 'These are dark times'. But objectively, it feels more like the world teeters at various brinks, as if the land beneath our feet has eroded without catching our attention. Here the species finds itself squashed onto what remains, those with the least, with the toes of their unshod feet dangling over the edge, while those with more sit comfortably in place, yet unaware that even their place isn't immune from attrition.

The world is littered with poor to outright terrible leaders, and many of them – personally – are doing just fine. So in the interest of fairness, I wanted to put it out there that you can – personally, if temporarily – achieve a measure of success while spending no time or energy in becoming a competent leader that people willingly follow.

It won't last mind you. . .

These leaders always end badly; their reigns of terror or apathy never last as long as they hope, their star never rises as high as they hope and – invariably – they end up isolated.

Because leadership has never really been just about being the kind of person people are willing to follow if you pay them enough. It's about being the kind of person people line up behind, beside and, when the moments call for it, in front of – even when it causes inconvenience, discomfort or personal pain.

You are disproportionately influential people in the lives of your people.

- Managers' impact on colleagues' mental health (69%) is more than that of doctors (51%) or therapists (41%)[1]
- Managers have just as much impact on colleagues' mental health as a spouse or partner (69%)[2]
- Work stress negatively impacts employees' home life (71%), well-being (64%), and relationships (62%)[3]
- 70% of the variance in the engagement of colleagues is the influence of their direct manager.[4]

It's YOU, you know – and I don't mean the collective you (accountability hides in the gaps between crowds), I mean you as an individual. What will you do?

Leadership isn't a role or a title, it's a promise of a kind of experience for your people – not that life will be easy or there will never be hardship. Instead, that challenge and support will be felt in equal measure – that credit will be applied to every link in the chain in success and everyone will bear the burden of failure together – that every voice and every person will be required to contribute. Every person, no matter their differences, their title or their agile working arrangement, will have space made for them to add value.

You are key to that – you are custodians of culture with an individual duty of care for the people around you. Being technically brilliant is not and will not be enough to stop the ongoing ceding of land to those who have already proven themselves disinterested in leadership.

You have seen that effective leadership is not magic.

It is built through commitment, presence, reflection, precision and the courage to act with integrity under pressure. These skills are ordinary – available to anyone willing to practise them with discipline.

SO what are you going to do?

If there is a solution to what ails this world, to the challenges in our businesses, institutions and communities, it's not 'the young people' – some distant, future generation or yet-to-be-discovered iconic future leader or politician.

In a second, I'll ask you to look up from this book and look around – the library, the park, the flat share, the dorm room or the office. Look beyond the windows and listen beyond the walls. Not one person you see or know to be there, but out of sight is the solution. The surest bet for any solution, remedy or balm for this world is YOU.

You won't be alone in this pursuit, but you will need to forge ahead initially at least, as if no change could be expected if it were left to anyone else. Then, you may naturally align with others who also took it upon themselves to be the change when no one around them did.

Be the leadership people need.

Be the support and challenge that drives performance and enables thriving.

Enable the team environment that will nurture talent and support innovation.

And remember always, sustainable change comes when enough people acknowledge:

It's not 'them'.
It's not 'we'.
It's you.

Some of you will have been told and now believe that 'nothing you do matters', that you are too small or inconsequential to make any real difference. This is a convenient lie for both those who tell it and those who hear it.

Those who tell you this lie want you to feel impotent and leave the status quo unchallenged. Those who hear it can feel better about their lack of effort or action, 'because what I might have done. . .' (whether that be vote, protest, run for office, intervene when you see non-optimal behaviour or demand that promotion), '. . .wouldn't have made a difference anyway'.

I don't need to know you to know that you make a difference. In my last book, I reminded you that 'everyone is a Giant to someone'. It won't take long if you scan your relationships to realise I'm telling you the truth.

Every day, you will have interactions with people that are inconsequential for you, and if you're not careful and vigilant, you will walk away, never knowing that your words or actions have had a profound impact on the people around you – rippling out into their lives.

Your words or actions embed themselves in their brains, like footprints in wet cement, destined to become part of the very foundation of how they think and behave in the future.

A former colleague told me this quote and made me promise to tell leaders whenever I got the chance, so I'm taking her advice and telling you:

'Your direct reports' children will know your name'.

Don't think yourself scot-free if you aren't a named manager; this quote is true for you in one context or another. Whether a teacher to their students, the experienced voice in the room to a new colleague, or because people see you at a distance, as a potential role model or just plain cool.

'Your direct reports' children will know your name'.

And they will know you either as the person who makes their parent, carer, partner or loved one feel sad, scared, angry, frustrated, small, stupid, insecure, irrelevant, incompetent or invisible, or they will know you as the person who challenges and supports their parent or carer, who makes them feel respected, capable, safe, confident, high-performing, cared for – and, yes, even happy.

What a remarkable obligation. And every day, with every interaction, what a wonderful opportunity.

I learned this lesson in 1995, playing for the Cleveland Cavaliers in my rookie year in the NBA. I was on a team that was so bad (they called it 'rebuilding') that I was a starter at the beginning of the season.

I lived in a hotel next to the Tower City Mall, which connected to Gund (now Rocket) arena, where the Cavs played. A fountain in that mall played music, and the water 'danced' in time. In the early season, between practice, weights and other duties, I would go there, usually head to toe in Cavs-emblazoned gear, always with a Sharpie in my pocket, hoping that someone would come up to me and ask for my autograph.

No one did.

That's how bad we must have been – that a prominent player, draped head to toe in Cavs gear, was near invisible. I don't remember any sneers or nasty remarks; I was simply unremarkable.

On one of these days, I had been sitting watching the fountain and realised it was time to leave. I stood to go, looked around and began to walk. A few steps in and from the corner of my eye, I saw a substantial Black woman barrelling through the crowd towards me, pulling her 13- or 14-year-old son behind her. From the resistance he was putting up and the look on his face peeking out behind her, he wanted nothing to do with this interaction – the seven-game losing streak to start the season probably didn't help.

When she arrived, she breathlessly but kindly asked if 'I'd sign this for my boy'. She thrust a used napkin from Panera Bread into my hand. I knew it was used because a generous smear of mayonnaise stuck it neatly to my palm.

I barely noticed or cared; this was my first public autograph (I wasn't counting team events where people came out for the stars and got me as a side dish).

I whipped out my Sharpie and signed my name, and instead of handing it to the mother, I reached around her and shook the boy's hand, then stuck the autograph neatly to his other palm.

I had done it! A personal autograph, more or less requested.

She said, 'Thank you!' I almost thanked her back before I regained my composure and walked away. This experience buoyed me, and as I briefly glanced back, the woman was attempting to bundle her son back through the crowd, but she could not.

The boy who had been so indifferent now stood legs locked, looking alternately from the hand I shook to the hand adorned with my mayonnaise autograph.

That was the moment for me. I was looking at me looking at him, realising that I was a bad basketball player on a bad team. Knowing I had weeks of hard evidence that no one else in Cleveland cared about my presence, and yet here was this kid looking at the hand I had shook as if he had been touched by God.

It was that moment that I realised that everyone is a Giant to someone – and that even if the majority don't care about or notice you, it doesn't take away from the profound opportunity to influence the few that may

That memory was a self-contained and enduring lesson in and of itself. That was until a random work day in the run-up to the London Olympics – 2010 or something like that – when I got an email via our generic website contact email.

I read it, and it was from the boy from the mall. He'd finished grad school and was a qualified psychologist.

He'd followed my career – the one that matters – and it had introduced him to psychology as a career. Attached to this email was a grainy picture of a yellowed mayonnaise autograph.

Those ripples, I told you about, really can be transformative.

It will not always be clear when you are standing at the threshold of someone else's defining memory. It will not always feel significant at the time.

But every word, every glance, every choice leaves an imprint – a memory that lingers, long after you have moved on.

Some of those memories will be told and retold, like family stories.

Others will be silent, unspoken, but will shape futures all the same.

Every day, whether you mean to or not, you are leaving marks on the lives of others.

That is the opportunity you have.

That is the responsibility you hold.

It has always been you.

It's still you.

It will always be you.

Choose to be the kind of Giant they deserve.

NOTES

INTRODUCTION

1. https://x.com/JohnAmaechi/status/1874820790438551667

CHAPTER 1

1. van der Meer, A. L. H., & van der Weel, F. R. (2024). Handwriting but not typewriting leads to widespread brain connectivity: Implications for learning and memory. *Frontiers in Psychology*, 15, Article 1219945. https://doi.org/10.3389/fpsyg.2023.1219945
2. Hollenbeck, J. R., Williams, K. J., & Klein, H. J. (1989). An empirical examination of the antecedents of commitment to difficult goals. *Journal of Applied Psychology*, 74(1), 18–23. https://doi.org/10.1037/0021-9010.74.1.18
3. Ryan, R. M., & Deci, E. L. (2000). Intrinsic and extrinsic motivations: Classic definitions and new directions. *Contemporary Educational Psychology*, 25(1), 54–67. https://doi.org/10.1006/ceps.1999.1020

4. Razak, L. A., Haliah, Habbe, A. H., Mediaty, & Arifuddin. (2020). Effect of framing and locus of control on commitment escalation in investment decision making. *Advances in Economics, Business and Management Research*, 92, 243–249.

5. Locke, E. A., & Latham, G. P. (2002). Building a practically useful theory of goal setting and task motivation: A 35-year odyssey. *American Psychologist*, 57(9), 705–717. https://doi.org/10.1037/0003-066X.57.9.705

6. Royer, H., Stehr, M., & Sydnor, J. (2015). Incentives, commitments and habit formation in exercise: Evidence from a field experiment with workers at a Fortune-500 company. *American Economic Journal: Applied Economics*, 7(3), 51–84. https://doi.org/10.1257/app.20130327

7. van der Meer, A. L. H., & van der Weel, F. R. (2024). Handwriting but not typewriting leads to widespread brain connectivity: Implications for learning and memory. *Frontiers in Psychology*, 15, Article 1219945. https://doi.org/10.3389/fpsyg.2023.1219945

CHAPTER 2

1. Eurich, T. (2018). What self-awareness really is (and how to cultivate it). Harvard Business Review, 4 January.

2. Ibid.

3. Yerkes, R. M., & Dodson, J. D. (1908). The relation of strength of stimulus to rapidity of habit-formation. *Journal of Comparative Neurology and Psychology*, 18(5), 459–482. https://doi.org/10.1002/cne.920180503

4. BBC News: https://www.bbc.co.uk/news/technology-49578400

5. There will likely be some debate about the use of this term being ableist. It isn't. Not only is there a literal blind spot in everyone's eye (fovea) where there are no light receptors, but it is widely accepted in the visually impaired community that this term is not related to vision.

6. Shelby, A. N. (1993). Organizational, business, management, and corporate communication: An analysis of boundaries and relationships. *Journal of Business Communication*, 30(3), 241–267. https://doi.org/10.1177/002194369303000304

CHAPTER 3

1. Bentley, T. G. K., D'Andrea-Penna, G., Rakic, M., Arce, N., LaFaille, M., Berman, R., Cooley, K., & Sprimont, P. (2023). Breathing practices for stress and anxiety reduction: Conceptual framework of implementation guidelines based on a systematic review of the published literature. *Brain Sciences*, 13(12): 1612. doi: 10.3390/brainsci13121612. PMID: 38137060; PMCID: PMC10741869.
2. Ahmed, A., Devi, R. G., & Priya, A. J. (2021). Effect of box breathing technique on lung function test. *Journal of Pharmaceutical Research International*, 33(58A), 25–31. doi: 10.9734/jpri/2021/v33i58A34085.
3. Bentley et al. (2023).
4. https://youtu.be/STVPxZWtaMk?si=10Iw2wP6wboO8a4k
5. Brahm, A. (2005). *Who Ordered This Truckload of Dung? Inspiring Stories for Welcoming Life's Difficulties*. Simon and Schuster.

CHAPTER 4

1. That is, trying to convey the dynamic interplay of opposing forces or contradictory elements within communication processes. This idea is rooted in dialectical theory, which examines how seemingly contradictory elements can coexist and interact in various aspects of life, including communication.
2. https://www.bbc.co.uk/programmes/b00729d9
3. Nikoleizig, L., Schmukle, S. C., Griebenow, M., & Krause, S. (2021). Investigating contributors to performance evaluations in small groups: Task competence, speaking time, physical expressiveness, and likability. *PLoS One*. 16(6), e0252980. doi: 10.1371/journal.pone.0252980. PMID: 34111193; PMCID: PMC8191988.

CHAPTER 5

1. Brown, B. (2012). *Daring Greatly: How the Courage to Be Vulnerable Transforms the Way We Live, Love, Parent, and Lead.* Penguin Random House Audio Publishing Group.
2. Wright, R. (2015). It's messy being authentic – lessons learned on the road to becoming an authentic leader. *Strategic HR Review,* 14 (3), 79–84. https://doi.org/10.1108/SHR-03-2015-0024
3. Williams, B. (2024). The role of psychological safety in enhancing radical candor and effective team dynamics. *IOSR Journal of Business and Management* 26 (11), 53–57. https://doi.org/10.9790/487x-2611135357.
4. Cho, H., Steege, L.M., & Arsenault Knudsen, É.N. (2023). Psychological safety, communication openness, nurse job outcomes, and patient safety in hospital nurses. *Research in Nursing and Health,* 46(4), 445–453. doi: 10.1002/nur.22327. Epub 2023 Jun 27. PMID: 37370217.
5. Sohail, S. H. (2024). Influence of authentic leadership on employee innovation and creativity in technology companies in Pakistan. *American Journal of Leadership and Governance,* 9, 1–13.
6. Baomar, S. M., and Islam, M. K. (2024). Evaluating the mediating role of transformational leadership in the nexus of employee motivation, engagement, emotional intelligence, and performance: A comprehensive review. *WSEAS Transactions on Business and Economics* 21 (August), 1713–1723. https://doi.org/10.37394/23207.2024.21.140.

CHAPTER 6

1. Brett, J., Staniszewska, S., Mockford, C., Herron-Marx, S., Hughes, J., Tysall, C., & Suleman, R. (2014). A systematic review of the impact of patient and public involvement on service users, researchers and communities. *The Patient: Patient-Centered Outcomes Research,* 7(4), 387–395. https://doi.org/10.1007/s40271-014-0065-0

2. Cuddy, A. J. C., Kohut, M., & Neffinger, J. (2013). Connect, then lead. *Harvard Business Review*, 91(7/8), 54–61.

3. https://www.plainenglish.co.uk/

4. https://literacytrust.org.uk/

5. http://gunning-fog-index.com/

6. https://readable.com/readability/history-of-readability/

7. The original source of this quote is Asimov, I. (1978). *My Own View*. In R. Holdstock (Ed.), *The Encyclopedia of Science Fiction* (pp. 10–11). London: Octopus Books. However, it was also featured in an epic episode of *Stargate SG-1*, in the show's 200th episode, titled '200', Season 10, Episode 6.

8. Zak, P. J. (2014. Why your brain loves good storytelling. *Harvard Business Review*, 28 October. https://hbr.org/2014/10/why-your-brain-loves-good-storytelling (accessed 1 June 2025).

9. Green, M. C., & Brock, T. C. (2000). The role of transportation in the persuasiveness of public narratives. *Journal of Personality and Social Psychology* 79(5), 701.

CHAPTER 7

1. Career Professionals of Canada (2022). Learning quotient (LQ): What it is, why it's important. 20 May. https://careerprocanada.ca/learning-quotient-lq-what-it-is-why-its-important/

CHAPTER 8

1. Simons, D. J., & Chabris, C. F. (1999). Gorillas in our midst: Sustained inattentional blindness for dynamic events. *Perception*, 28(9), 1059–1074. https://doi.org/10.1068/p281059

2. Detert, J. R., & Edmondson, A. C. (2011). Implicit voice theories: Taken-for-granted rules of self-censorship at work. *Academy of Management Journal*, 54(3), 461–488. https://doi.org/10.5465/amj.2011.61967925
3. Nemeth, C. J., Connell, J. B., Rogers, J. D., & Brown, K. S. (2001). Improving decision making by means of dissent. *Journal of Applied Social Psychology*, 31(1), 48–58. https://doi.org/10.1111/j.1559-1816.2001.tb02481.x
4. Morrison, E. W. (2014). Employee voice and silence. *Annual Review of Organizational Psychology and Organizational Behavior*, 1(1), 173–197. https://doi.org/10.1146/annurev-orgpsych-031413-091328

CHAPTER 9

1. Schön, D. A. (1992). *The Reflective Practitioner: How Professionals Think in Action* (1st ed.). Routledge. https://doi.org/10.4324/9781315237473

CHAPTER 10

1. Peterson, R. A. (2000). *Constructing Effective Questionnaires*. Thousand Oaks, CA: Sage.
2. Sherman, J. W., & Allen, T. J. (2011). Ego threat and intergroup bias: A test of the Motivated Activation Hypothesis. *Psychological Science*, 22(3), 331–333. https://doi.org/10.1177/0956797611399291; Jost, J. T., & Hunyady, O. (2005). Antecedents and consequences of system-justifying ideologies. *Current Directions in Psychological Science*, 14(5), 260–265. https://doi.org/10.1111/j.0963-7214.2005.00377.x; Van den Bos, K., & Lind, E. A. (2010). The social psychology of fairness and the regulation of personal uncertainty. In R. M. Arkin, K. C. Oleson, & P. J. Carroll (Eds.), *Handbook of the Uncertain Self* (pp. 122–141). New York: Psychology Press.

3. Ibarra, H. (1999). Provisional selves: Experimenting with image and identity in professional adaptation. *Administrative Science Quarterly*, 44(4), 764–791.

EPILOGUE

1. UKG Workforce Institute (2023). *Mental Health at Work: Managers and Money*. Lowell, MA: UKG. https://www.ukg.com/sites/default/files/2023-01/CV2040-Part2-UKG%20Global%20Survey%202023-Manager%20Impact%20on%20Mental%20Health-FINAL.pdf
2. Ibid.
3. Ibid.
4. Gallup, Inc. (2015). *State of the American Manager: Analytics and Advice for Leaders*. Washington, DC.: Gallup. https://m100group.com/wp-content/uploads/2015/07/stateofamericanmanager_0515_mh_lr.pdf

ACKNOWLEDGEMENTS

With my wholehearted thanks to:

Dr Michelle Mahdon, without whom this book wouldn't be. Your incisive assessment of me made all the difference and was the catalyst that opened my eyes to the possibility of this book.

The APS Intelligence team for supporting me while writing this book; their patience with me as the deadline loomed has been nothing less than magnificent.

The Wiley editors for their patience and thoughtfulness in editing this book.

My colleagues at the University of Exeter Business School for their faith in and support of me.

The many colleagues whose content I've consumed online and at conferences over the last year, and whose work has generated so many new questions and ideas.

My family and friends, who managed and supported me through moments of frazzledom. I only made it because of you.

And perhaps most of all, to my fellow and future Giants. The world, whether of work or more broadly, won't change for the better without you.

ABOUT
THE AUTHOR

Professor John Amaechi OBE is one of the most compelling thinkers on leadership and organisational culture working today. A respected psychologist, best-selling author and founder of APS Intelligence, he has spent over two decades helping leaders navigate complexity with clarity, purpose and courage. His work challenges conventional wisdom, revealing how power is enacted, how trust is earned or lost, and why skill and integrity must sit at the heart of influence.

John is a Chartered Psychologist, a Chartered Scientist and a Professor of Leadership at the University of Exeter Business School. His credentials span psychology, human resources, and applied science and technology, and he is recognised through fellowships and chartered status with leading professional bodies in the UK, Canada and Australia – a rare cross-disciplinary honour that reflects both depth and practical relevance.

John's first book, *Man in the Middle* (2007), offered an unvarnished look at identity and ambition, chronicling his journey as the first Briton to play in the NBA. His later work, *The Promises of Giants* (2021), became a leadership essential, urging those in positions of influence to act with humanity, rigour and purpose. His writing has also featured in influential reports and anthologies exploring leadership ethics, social justice and the power of sport to drive societal change, including *More Than a Game,* a Centre for Social Justice report on the shortcomings and potential of sport policy, *Connected Worlds,* a volume for public sector leaders on courageous and values-driven leadership, and Baroness Grey-Thompson's *Duty of Care in Sport* report to the UK Government.

In every setting, John brings a rare combination of scientific acuity, ethical clarity and a captivating storytelling approach. He speaks when truth is needed – especially when it is inconvenient – and invites those with power not just to perform, but to lead with intention, skill and a deep sense of responsibility.

INDEX